PKT . 22-96

VOICES

FROM

DOWNSTREAM

by

Phil F. Carspecken, Jr.

Published by

Wainsley Press

ISBN 0-9653988-3-8

Printed in the United States

For any information please contact
Wainsley Press
P.O. Box 546
Nevada, MO 64772
(417) 667-4703

DEDICATION

To Margaret—soul mate and invaluable inspirer/editor.

And to our children: Kathleen, Christine, Phil III, and Randy.

These are the most beloved of all the many "Voices from Downstream".

ACKNOWLEDGEMENT

For the cover artwork, the author thanks Bob Pils, master artist, master of the art of fly-fishing, and master of many other arts of living.

FOREWORD

In my early childhood, I was wonder-struck about many things in the world around me. But I probably wasn't word-struck until my seventh year.

In the second-grade chapter of my life, my mother and sister and I spent a wintry interlude with an aunt and her family in Oklahoma. My father, who had deep feelings and a fine talent for expressing them, wrote us a lonesome-sounding letter from our Iowa home. He commented on the emptiness of the household, bereft of the three of us, and as I read his moving words, tears welled in my eyes.

It was then that a new wonder hit me, head-on: My father, many miles away, had written some words that travelled far to reach us. And when I read my father's words, they made me cry. "Words," I thought, "just plain *words*, made me cry!"

That was the moment in my life when the wonder of words took charge! And I eventually came to discover the excitement of hunting down those symbols that capture the uncapturable; the thrill of finding the most precise word, the finest-sounding word, the word that best blends with the flow, the *extraordinary* word! And I later learned—and must still continue to remind myself—that oftentimes, ordinary words do better than extraordinary ones.

A junior high English teacher of mine read one of my themes to our class. At the end of a sentence that described a porcupine "shambling along the shoreline," she paused and said, "Notice, class, that Phil didn't just say that the porcupine walked; he said that it *shambled*." And she threw me a warmly approving smile. That symbol for a slow, clumsy gait propelled me into a smooth, upward stride—and at that higher altitude I gained some sorely needed confidence...and the notion that maybe, someday, I'd be able to write for a living—become a professional "hunter-gatherer of words," as I now call myself. During my adult life, and up to that teacher's final year, she always received a grateful Christmas message from a former pupil!

What a great challenge it is to plunk myself down before my typewriter, reel in a snowy and empty word-vessel, hunch into a somewhat prayerful position, and then reach out for that brimming treasury of over half-a-million English words to try and pin down a wispy idea that's been stirring through my mind! To "let your fingers do the walking" over the keyboard in eager pursuit of the best way to say something—*that* is a peak experience!

It has been my dominant instinct to write about "cabbages" rather than "kings"—to consider the musings of ordinary folk rather than the machinations of the high and the mighty and the sinister—to focus on pacific ponderings rather than rip-roaring perils. I've known no desire to set my pages aflame with torrid sex, nor to riddle them with slashing violence. I gravitate toward amusing, memorable and awe-inspiring things. I like to spell out, as best I can, sensations that sometimes dawn upon us at daybreak, and that linger like the sunset afterglow.

More and more in this autumnal (early winter?) stage of life, I think about that line from "Knickerbocker Holiday," "when the days dwindle down to a precious few". I think about Richard Rodger's statement, written late in his career: "The sweetest sounds I've ever heard are still within my head." I think about the fragmented trains of thought, still jumbled within my mental freight-yard; formless feelings yet to be delineated, strung meaningfully together, and sent out along the rails. Oh, I probably have another decade left—maybe two— in which to sort out that chaotic scramble. But, time is passing!

Then there's that baffling question: "What *is* time?" I've struggled with the astro-physicists' view of that mysterious dimension, and I inevitably fall back to a simple, earth-bound metaphor. Time, for me, is a stream, forever flowing from unknown headwaters toward an unknown confluence. The moving waters are sometimes tranquil, sometimes turbulent. They flow ceaselessly, inexorably. And they heed us not.

From our finite points along an infinite shore, we ephemeral beings peer upstream to wonder what is drifting our way. When joyful interludes arrive, we yearn to reach into the eternal flow to seize and hold them—but they sweep on past to vanish downstream.

Yet, even though cherished moments rush relentlessly by, we are endowed with the ability to continue hearing the voices —sometimes muted, sometimes in crescendo—enabling us to recapture the wonder, and excitement, and exultation.

The voices will speak to us more clearly if, throughout our brief existence, we quicken our senses to discover the uncommon in the commonplace, the heroic in the humdrum— the visions, chords and flavors that too often pass us by unseen, unheard, and unsavored.

This is the unifying thread within the fabric of these reminiscences, observations, and ponderings. The downstream voices whisper, shout, and chuckle about many different things:

- Searching for a constellation, lost somewhere in the astral wilderness.
- Reliving the moment when a wild creature swam by on sightless course to vanish in the rain, and remain forever in memory.
- Gazing through a ghostly gateway to recapture a bright vision.
- Revisiting a campsite along a wild river, to hear phantom voices from decades downstream.
- Marveling at a sacred glow that sometimes breaks upon us with the dawn.

- Enjoying again the laughter-stirring, wonder-stirring fragments of time that continue to bring enrichment.

Thus the unifying strand meanders through these pages, connecting with enduring points of time that loom out of the grey and trail off like a vivid row of fence posts toward the skyline.

Such are the rewards for those who are alive to all the miraculous within the present...and to the many, haunting *Voices from Downstream*.

TABLE OF CONTENTS

FOREWORD vii

VOICES FROM THE FAMILY CIRCLE 1
The Kid in the Bow 3
So Please Remember 9
Revelation in the Rain 11
"Weak" Vacation 15
The Lost Constellation 18
Of Birds and Bees and DNA 24
Gateway to Somewhere 27
Perils of Parenting 32
Voices from Downstream 35

VOICES FROM THE WILD PLACES 41
Tenting on the Old Campground 43
"Now is the Winter of Our Discontent" 50
Roaming the Sundown Territory 53
The Trail to Sanctuary 58
The Morning Show 61
"Making a Little Difference..." 63
Coming Inside the Stockade 66

VOICES FROM CULTIVATED FIELDS 69
"Songs My Mother Taught Me..." 71
Words About Words 74
Stalking A Subject 77
"The Melody Lingers On" 80
Stay Tuned to the Book Network 83
Weavings from Empty Looms 86
Good Bye, Mitch—You Left us "Dreaming of a Song" 89
Beware of "Jargonitis" 91
The Greatest Idea Since the Wheel 94

VOICES FROM THE TRAFFIC STREAM 97
The Guy in the Other Lane 99
Gliding Through the Gelderland 101
The Eighth Wonder of the World 107
The Peddling of Pedaling 109
The Children Who Bloom in the Spring 112
The Case of the Unparallel Parker 113
Two-Wheeled & Four-Wheeled Tour de France . . . 115
Soliloquy of a Highway Hamlet 117

VOICES FROM DEEPER CURRENTS 119
Unfinished Symphony 121
Hunters in the Night 122
Keeping a Religious Sensitivity 125
Sleep Well, O Kindred Spirit 131
On "Getting Religion" 133
The View from "Lookout Point" 137

VOICES FROM THE LIGHTER SIDE 139
The Latitude of Attitude 141
Adventures in Film Making - One 144
Adventures in Film Making - Two 147
Off the Top of My Head 150
Posters Post Vivid Memories 152
The Struggle Toward Organization 155
Spaced Out in Cyberspace 157

VOICES FROM RANDOM TRIBUTARIES 161
A Significant Sunrise 163
"What's in a Name?" 165
The Management of Morning 168
"First, You Get Married!" 171
"To Sleep...Perchance to Dream" 173
Inner Thoughts Along the Inner Passage 176
Class Reunions—A Time for All Birds to Sing 179
For a Buoyant Body and Soul 182

VOICES FROM CHRISTMAS PAST 185
   "...If Only in My Dreams" 187
   Shifting Into the Goodwill Gear 191
   Re-Awakening 193
   Transformation 195
   The Christmas Quest 196
   Grace for Christmas 197
   Angel Chimes 198

AFTERWORD 201

VOICES FROM

THE FAMILY CIRCLE

THE KID IN THE BOW

I leaned forward eagerly in the bow as the canoe glided out of the bay. We rounded the point, and the main waters of Lake Saganaga came into view. It was "Big Sag" all right—so big that her islands faded off into the hazy distance, and her wild shoreline ran on and on into the north, tapering down to a slender thread. It was an awe-inspiring sight for a ten-year old. I was the happiest kid this side of Hudson Bay!

It had been an eternity, waiting until I would be old enough to join Dad's North Woods gang. How I had pored over his maps of the Quetico-Superior, and thrilled to tales of his yearly canoe jaunts! Now it was another spring...another plunge into wilderness canoe country...and *I* was part of the gang!

We headed northward, Dad and I and the three in the other canoe, and for me there was pure adventure in every shadowy bay and every foot of shoreline. But even greater adventure awaited us up ahead. We were trolling for trout through the deep narrows when suddenly my heart leaped as Dad dropped his paddle and grabbed his rod.

"A strike! I've got one, Flip! Better reel in your line!"

I reeled away furiously while staring in fascination at Dad's sharply bent rod. I thirsted for sight of the fish, but it seemed an endless time before Dad could work him near the surface.

"He's coming up," Dad said as he stiffened in expectation, reeling steadily. I peered into the blue water for a first glimpse. But suddenly the reel screamed as he lunged again for the depths.

Finally the fighting trout began to tire. His runs became shorter and weaker. Dad was reeling constantly now, and then I sighted a glint of silver, deep down but circling upward. He was a fair-sized trout, but to a youngster who had seen nothing but pan fish, he was the largest monster that ever sprouted fins.

Dad started to work him alongside the canoe. All the scrap seemed to have left him. He hung quietly on the surface, his tail flicking slightly back and forth. When he drifted temptingly close to the bow, an idea flashed into my head. Impulsively I shot out a hand and grabbed him behind the gills. He was a lot of slippery weight, but thanks to a determined heave and to beginner's luck, the trout was soon flopping in the bottom of the canoe.

My hands were cold and slimy and my pants were soaking with the water that had cascaded in with the catch. But inside, I was all aglow! I glanced at Dad and his startled expression quickly gave way to a grin flashing warmly behind his pipe. "Well, by George," was all he could summon—and I was enjoying the greatest triumph of my young life!

"Well, fellas," Dad said at the campfire that night, "I'd always told Flip that the real sport was hauling 'em in by hand, and the heck with a gaff or dip net. But I didn't expect him to take a stab at it so soon. We're quite a team. I hook 'em and he lands 'em."

The ruddy fire's warmth was nothing compared with the warmth that I found in those words. I belonged! I was part of a team!

Since I was knee-high to a casting rod, Dad and I had shared much together—romping in the backyard, pitching horseshoes, tramping through the Iowa timber. But in the Quetico-Superior wilderness, far over the horizon from roads, resorts, and outboards, I came to see my father as I had never seen him before. Our companionship grew stronger. The team that was formed that memorable spring went on to many a wilderness adventure, deeply influencing my life.

Our canoeing trips became as regular as the spring breakup. I had much to learn in the earlier years, but I had a patient teacher. I soon knew how to rig up a casting rod, and how to whip out a lure without snagging the seat of my pants. I learned that you can't "horse in" a big fish with an 18-pound test line, that you must beware of a walleye's sharp dorsal fin, that somehow, you can always manage to reach the end of the most hopeless backlash.

I discovered many things through blood-tingling experience! How the day stands out when I *hooked* my first fish, as well as landed it. I was casting an old, scarred bass plug from a rocky point—an unlikely spot for northern pike. The object was casting practice, with no thought of a catch.

But I felt a sharp tug that sent the blood pounding in my ears. My yell echoed from shore to shore. Dad, at camp just around the bend, thought I must have flushed a bear. He was soon panting at my side, and he was a welcome sight. I was a rattled angler who needed help badly.

"Give him line," was his first command, for my fingers were frozen on the reel and my rod threatened to become a hangman's noose. The reel shrieked as the fish plunged out. "Now snap on your brake," and the calm voice persuaded me to start breathing again. He showed me how to keep the spring of the rod against the pull of the fish, and told me when to reel up on him and when to let him run. Before long I was fairly well in command of things, thanks to assuring coaching.

The northern soon tuckered out and I drew him close to the point. "Be ready to let him rip if he's got another dash in him," Dad warned. But there was no more dash. "Now grab him behind the gills, just like you did that trout. He's all yours, Flip." I knelt down, gripped, and out came the dripping prize. He was just a six-pounder, but he could have been a 40-pound lunker for the pride that tingled up and down my frame!

They filmed us—Dad and me and my first catch. But even without this record, the experience would stand out today like a monarch pine in a stand of poplar! And it's not merely the excitement of it all; it's a sense, too, of a father being there with ready guidance in a tight spot.

Not all the impressive experiences came at the business end of a fishing rod. Take "Dead Man's Portage"—an endless, mosquito-clouded test of human mettle. I tackled it with a grub pack, and with a lot of zest, for portages were adventure, too. But halfway through the torturous trip, adventure had simmered down to sweat...and dangerously close to tears.

I had fallen far behind the gang, and felt deserted and abused. When I staggered to the end of the portage, I was at the end of my rope. Dad was loading our canoe. He grinned at me, but I didn't have a single smile within me. I was swinging my pack out to him when a mosquito began drilling my nose. I dropped my pack to clobber the pest, ripping off a lumberjack oath. The canoe nearly swamped and I gave Dad a sheepish glance. "Pretty tough portage, son," he quietly said, "but take a look at that lake. A clean breeze out there, and no bugs. Campsite's about a mile up, on the left shore."

Shame was swelling inside of me when I climbed into the bow. Dad had taken three trips on that portage. The bugs had chewed him just as badly. He was just as hungry and tired—but his outlook was as fresh as morning! He was seeing sparkling water and an intriguing shoreline, and I was seeing muck and mosquitoes. It was a lesson without preaching, and it sank in.

There were also days of steady rain—pushing up the lake against the slashing downpour, gingerly trying your footing on slippery boulders with the pack's straps biting into your shoulders, pitching camp on a soggy site and coaxing a fire to start. Sometimes, when Dad and I would look at each other in our dripping ponchos, he'd chuckle and say, "Flip, if your mother could see you now!" And I'd grin at him through the downpour. I'd found a kind of thrill in keeping my head up in the rain.

One unforgettable day we were running a dangerous track down a river, aiming to veer into the portage at the head of a falls. I was paddling mightily in the bow and didn't see a submerged rock dead ahead. Suddenly there was a sickening scrape. The canoe halted sharply, then began to pivot on the rock in the swift current, with the falls roaring just below. Fear surged through me as I turned and looked in panic at Dad in the stern. His face was grim, but he shouted above the snarling water, "We'll get out of this! Sit tight!"

Dad stepped out into the swirl of rapids onto a slippery rock. He freed us with a series of heaves. We started drifting toward the brink, but he scrambled back into the stern and we pulled madly for the inlet. Soon the spray and pounding waters were behind us as we lunged into quiet water. We sat at the landing, limp but triumphant, panting and grinning at each other. The team had botched one, but came through.

Evening campfires are the richest of wilderness experiences. In a youngster's eyes, a fire is a daub of brightness in a universe of dark; it is a fragrant blend of wood smoke and pipe smoke, a circle of glowing warmth containing many a rousing story and song. There was fascination in the leaping flames, and when a loon's call would suddenly shatter the silence, I'd wriggle closer to the embers...and closer to Dad's side.

But the most tender memory of all is the time when the evening chow had been tucked away and the camp chores were done. Then, as the shadows began to reach far out upon the lake, I would eagerly await "the word." In the midst of the chatter around the fire, Dad would glance into the west, then turn to me and say, "Flip, it's time we were slipping down the shoreline."

Quick as a chipmunk I'd grab my rod and the paddles and dash for the canoe. We would shove off into the spell of evening over the lake—into the most vivid experience of my life. We landed some good ones along those dusky shores, but best of all I remember the magic of twilight over a wilderness lake...the silhouette of the western shore in the sunset...the soft plunk of paddles and the musical tinkle of water trickling from the blades...the evening song of the hermit thrush, ringing out in the silence...the enchantment of that fleeting time between dusk and darkness.

A wonderful father-son relationship is born in rugged, under-the-sky life together. A sparkling-eyed "kid in the bow" inherits balsam-scented dreams and memories...patience and staying power when trails get tough...a widened vision that keeps his eyes lifted to the highest range of hills.

Today, the wilderness team is—in a sense—broken. The father has the spirit, but the years have become too many for the demands of the canoe journeys. But he has the bright flood of memories, and in his den is a huge map of the Quetico-Superior territory, where all his routes and campsites are marked. In his mind's eye the vast waters still sparkle in the sun...the cedars still glisten in the mist of Louisa Falls...the campfires still blaze from islands and rugged points.

As for the former kid in the bow, someday he may be heading north again. But I think he might hit a new chain of lakes rather than the old ones.

Why? Because there would be something forlorn about the old camps, and a somber hue in the evening fires on Lake Agnes, beside Kenebas Falls, or on the huge rock slab at Kawnipi. Because when he'd slip out into twilight along those familiar shorelines, there'd be a haunting sadness in that thrush song ringing through the solitude, and greyish gloom would steal in amidst the shadows.

Because, out there in the sacred stillness, he would once again become the tender kid in the bow—and he would be lonely there in the wilderness dusk.

SO PLEASE REMEMBER...

Whenever I think of that morning, the same feeling of pride and the same heart twinge return. You whirled in excitement on the walk, trim and dainty in your "extra special" dress. You glanced up at the porch and smiled at your mother and me, your blonde hair gleaming in the September morning sunlight. You were an inexpressible blend of fast-growing girl and tender child that morning, poised in readiness to bound off to your first day of kindergarten.

Karen was a forlorn little doll, lying in the corner of your room. I noticed her there when your mother was brushing your hair. Karen's going to fall from your favor now, I thought. Oh, you won't shut her out completely, but she'll suffer increasing neglect as you plunge into new adventures with letters, and numbers, and words, and stars, and rainbows, and the moon. Karen's world will soon vanish in the wake of your eager, expanding steps.

You're heading into a much wider world, I reflected. And I guess it's a selfish ache we feel, deep down inside, as we watch you skipping through its portal. That freckle-sprinkled nose of yours will lead you into some great and joyous times in the school years ahead of you. And you'll discover shadows of sorrow and bewilderment, too, interlaced with the sunshine.

The first peal of the school bell rang out in the crisp air. You squared your small shoulders and set out, hopping along airily in your new shoes. And when you turned to wave goodbye to us, I wanted to say some tender things—to express tender thoughts and feelings welling up from deep inside. But all that I could force past that lump in my throat was "So long, Kathleen...and don't forget to look both ways."

There are all kinds of motorists—all kinds of people—in this world, Kathleen. There are many good ones, and few who mean you any harm. But—one breed is bent on saving seconds of time, for reasons even they couldn't explain. Their thinking is confined within the sphere of the almighty speedometer. They load all responsibilities upon your frail shoulders—their own, along with those that you should rightfully bear. They "haven't time" to grant you the margin of safety that every child deserves.

There's the hazard, too, in stepping off the curb of conformity. Bruising experiences often await those who have the courage to be themselves—who are strong enough individuals to refuse trailing blindly along with the herd.

It is a BIG step from the tranquil side streets of childhood out into the main thoroughfares. It is a wonderful, promising, limitless highway...and yet it can also lead to unexpected collisions with insensitivity, envy, cruelty, even danger. How does a parent build trust in human goodness, while also developing a constant awareness for the sinister few who cannot be trusted? How much danger and pain can we spare our children, and how much must they endure through first-hand experience?

It is perhaps a parent's most agonizing moment when their child is poised at the curb, ready to step out into the mainstream. Are they ready? Have we done our *very* best to prepare them? ·

And the burning thought that emerges from the welter of hopes and doubts and pride and fear is, "Please remember, Kathleen,—always—to look both ways!"

REVELATION IN THE RAIN

It was a day in my boyhood, filled with wind and rain—and with an experience that made me begin to see the world in a different light.

We were paddling northward, Dad and I, through a slate-grey morning in Canadian canoe country. As we approached a narrows midway up the lake, a curtain of rain swished down from the north to meet us. We wriggled into foul-weather gear and headed on toward a distant campsite.

It wasn't bad, paddling through the rain. Soggy days, mosquitoes, tough portages—these were tests administered by a stern but kindly Mother Nature.

There had been times of doubt: moments in the night when the loon cry shivered to crescendo; a creature's scream in the talons of an owl; nights of storm with pines lashed by surges of wind and the tent flapping in agony.

But storms would end. Nature would once more smile with gentle warmth, pleased at the way I had weathered her wrath.

So, as we bore down on the narrows, I found a thrill in riding into the slash of wind and rain. I turned and grinned at Dad in the stern, and he winked over his upside-down pipe. I then resumed paddling with all the enthusiasm of youth.

It happened in the heart of the narrows—there where the sheer walls of rock, splashed with surrealistic orange and a strange blue, plunged down from great height. I was peering through this canyon, eager to sight the main body of the lake, water sloshing from my hat brim with each stroke. Then I saw something far ahead on the water. "Something's up ahead," I half whispered. We rested paddles and peered into the slanting rain.

It was only a lone beaver swimming our way. But we sat tight, drifting in the wind gusts that bullied through the canyon.

We were curious to see how close he'd come before he smacked the water with his tail and dived.

But this beaver didn't fit the normal pattern. Onward he swam, bearing down on us head-on. Excitement began to build as the solitary swimmer steadily narrowed the gap between us. He was bigger than any beaver I'd ever seen. And he was old.

A paddle's length off the bow, he paused in confusion. He turned in an uncertain half-circle, milled slowly about, then hung in the water as though waiting for us to make the next move.

All at once he lunged upward in strange desperation, pointing his snout directly at me. I looked at his scarred head, at his eyes...and then I understood. The milky eyes peered at me with transparent stare. "He's blind!" I said. But the wind tore my words away. Silently in the cold rain we watched him turn away and thread his sightless course down the narrows, with small white caps now and then sloshing up to blot him from view. At last he faded into the curtain of rain...and with him faded all my childish illusions about a kindly nature —about the whole scheme of things!

We swung into the north again. There was a cruel sting in the rain, and the wind leered at us and our frail canoe. There was something frightening in the barren sweep of lake and the rock walls towering over us. I took a last look at the empty expanse where the lone traveler had disappeared. And I shuddered.

I needed to talk it out, though I didn't want to. But there was no time for talk.

The wind, though dying, still tormented the pines as we sat by our campfire that night. I huddled close to the flames—a speck of light in a sea of darkness—seeking a warmth I couldn't find.

"Tough break for that beaver, to lose its sight," Dad said.

I nodded, staring into the fire.

"But he's still hanging on; still got his other senses, and his strength.   Notice how he kept his head up and swam right on? An animal loses its sight, or a leg, but it keeps on going, long as there's life."

"But—to be blind, and so...so all alone," I said.

Dad sensed my fear and confusion.   "Nature's so far beyond us, son, that we'll never understand all her ways. She's as close as the ground at our feet, and she goes on forever beyond the Milky Way.

"Like that beaver, we've pretty much got to shift for ourselves.   That's the way it has to be, for free beings. Animals go it mostly alone, but we humans have learned a lot about giving each other a hand.   And you'll come to understand that we're lucky to have tough going now and then. Smooth sailing doesn't develop muscle; doesn't develop character; doesn't develop anything worthwhile.

"Seems like we have to know pain to know happiness.   To enjoy life's wonderful things, and its freedom, we have to accept its risks.   Sure, blindness is a terrible thing—but then we have intelligence to help prevent blindness, and kindness to help those who do lose their sight.   Blind humans don't have to go it all alone, like that beaver."

As Dad talked quietly on, the wind whispered down into silence and stars began to show.   Wisps of reconciliation began to come...began to mingle with my fear and bewilderment... began to drive away some of the oppressive gloom.

I didn't realize it then, but the foundation was partially laid that night for more sober and enduring beliefs.   For a spell as I lay in my blankets, I thought of the sightless beaver— remembering the stony stare...wondering where he was out there in the blackness...wondering how he'd manage when winter came snarling over the lakes and hills.   But sleep finally came.

In the succeeding days and months, those milky eyes often appeared to haunt me—especially before I dropped off to sleep at night. Always, those sightless eyes were pleading for help, asking for guidance through those rugged narrows...through the wilderness...through a starkly solitary life.

But my sensitive father's words beside the campfire that memorable night took root in my mind, and they flourished with time. Gradually, more realistic concepts took shape and began to grow where tender fancy had been rudely brushed away. The jagged edges of the memory were gradually worn smooth in the incessant flow of time. I came to think less of the milky eyes and more of the way the creature had forged stoically on to vanish in the rain. I came to sense an unflinching courage, a wild and wonderful freedom.

Now, looking back on that day of painful revelation, I still feel a faint twinge. But it's also like suddenly coming upon a new lake and standing on the windswept shore, gazing into the bluish sweep where the white caps are breaking crisp and clean. The same, wild bigness is there, mingled with humility and soaring thankfulness for *life* with its risk and opportunity—its potential for tragedy and triumph—its unknown tomorrow of darkness or of splendid light.

"WEAK" VACATION

When our third child began to signal that arrival was imminent, our well-laid plans went operational. I had arranged for a week off work to run the household and monitor our two small daughters during my spouse's confinement.

I was fairly confident about keeping the home fires aglow and overseeing the whirlwind action of our high-spirited daughters, Kathleen and Christine. I could be stern—well, sort of—if necessary. I could cook—well, brew coffee, make toast, open cereal boxes, cans, milk bottles—things like that.

But while I was reasonably competent with stove, fridge, can opener, toaster and vacuum cleaner, I'd had no washing machine experience. On my second morning of solo parenting, after puzzling over Bendix buttons and dials, I launched a load of laundry. The machine hummed to life, and beyond its little, round window, a sudsy scene appeared. "You're a laudable launderer," I bragged. But later, when the spin-dry cycle ended, there was no dry. The sodden stuff just huddled there, submerged in water that was supposed to have been magically spun away.

"Know what Mommie does when that happens?" Kathleen asked as I stared at the recalcitrant machine. "No, what?" "She opens the funny little door down there and does something." "Really? You're sure it's *that* funny little door, and not another one?" "That's the one," she said. So I opened the door, and when my groping fingers felt something cylindrical, I gave it a tentative twist. Instantly, a mini Johnstown flood of water gushed forth. I was so stunned that I didn't even swear...just then. I grabbed towels, a sweat shirt, everything dry that was at hand, and started mopping.

After bailing out the utility room, I called my hospitalized spouse for some washing machine orientation, and then took another stab at laundry duty. This time the balky Bendix spurned water and began galloping into a dry wash—until a very costly "crrraaaack" exploded through the atmosphere when the agitator split stem to stern. "Hold the laundry 'til I get home!" was the next telephonic instruction from the hospital.

Then there were those fiery spats between our little lasses that suddenly shattered the calm. I'd rush in like an NFL referee, yelling in as commanding a tone as I could muster that "the next one who starts a fight gets thrown out of the game!" But in spite of intense listening and spying on their interaction, I could never spot the spat-starter. The wrangling just came, "Kerwhammm," like a thunderbolt out of the blue.

One afternoon after a stint of outdoor play, one daughter and a neighborhood lad emerged from a dense clump of trees in our backyard. When I greeted them, something about their appearance sent a disquieting signal. There was something unorthodox...something strange...something WRONG! She was wearing little boy clothes; he was wearing little girl clothes. "Omigawd, they've switched," I said to my shocked self. "Our little girl's on the brink of ruin, and I'm facing the crisis alone!"

"Uh," I gasped, "nice kids don't do that—get undressed, I mean, and switch clothes. It's too—uh—it's against the rules!" I fumbled through a clothing switchback, shooed the boy home, then rushed to the phone for more emergency advice from the maternity ward. Surprisingly, Margaret took the stunning news lightly. "I've kept telling you those trees should be thinned out," she chuckled.

After those l-o-n-g "vacation" days came the bedtime story endurance contest. Oh, those grueling times with Willie Whale and Tommy Turtle! A short way into the electrifying plot and undynamic dialogue had me dozing off, until I'd feel a nudge and hear a faint voice penetrating from the sleep-fog: "Go on Daddy. Then what happened?" So I'd plunge again into the storyless story line, fighting to keep the sag out of my sagging eyelids.

One evening I had fought mightily through the unadventures of Bozo the Clown, succumbing to overpowering slumber, reviving to struggle through a few more soporific sentences, then drifting off again into oblivion. I finally droned to the end of the puny plot, tucked the girls in, crooned a few of their favorite songs, kissed them, murmured a semiconscious wish for pleasant dreams, and staggered out to collapse on the couch.

Minutes—perhaps hours—later, the doorbell partially awakened me. I wended a woozy way down the hall to discover a briefcase-armed gentleman at the threshold. Too numb to say "Sorry, not interested," I let him talk his persuasive way into the living room where he went into a well-polished intro, then opened his briefcase. I have a fuzzy recollection of him, brandishing a brochure or two...and that's when I must have zonked out.

Minutes—perhaps hours—later, I came to, glanced around, and was startled to find myself alone. The stranger had folded his briefcase and silently stolen away, leaving his prospect in "a deep dream of peace."

Ever since, I've often wondered who that guy was, and what he was trying to sell.

THE LOST CONSTELLATION

On a long, late-night trip home after a business meeting, half asleep in the car's back seat, I began scanning the stars visible through the side window. I soon spotted the Pole Star, then tracked down the light years along the curve of the Big Dipper's handle.

Ursa Major—the silvery spectacle swept me back to the star-studded years of my childhood. There were impossible distances between my father's forefinger and the constellations, but he had led me clear out there to the gleaming neighborhoods of Orion, Cassiopeia's Chair, the Pleiades, The Seven Sisters—or were the Sisters and the Pleiades the same? It'd been a long time since I'd roamed the interstellar spaces.

So star-struck was I in my childhood that each constellation revealed a wispy, individual presence. Andromeda wore cloudy robes of tragedy. Venus radiated an armless kind of beauty. The Pleiades were clustered in a bright nebula of sisterhood. And my inner ear sometimes seemed to hear celestial music descending through the night—ethereal currents of harmony, flashing and fading like the Northern Lights; half-real melody, like the scarcely-seen seventh sister of the Pleiades.

Then the memory of "The Diamond" constellation flashed into my mind. How could I have forgotten about it, I wondered, as I began searching for it. Was it high in the northeast? Or low in the southeast? I wasn't sure, and I searched in vain that night from the moving car.

I remembered "The Diamond" as small and dim, but the night of its discovery flared with meteor-brilliance in my memory: star-strewn sky, a ghostly spiral of campfire smoke, stretches of stillness stitched by the distant riffle of Flint Creek, the feeling of solemnity under the vast arch of sky, and the warmth of earth and woolen blankets.

Dad was smoking a final pipe as we lay in our bedrolls. Our course was arrow-straight from earthen launch pad to the furthest astral borders. We gazed through the vastness, building the "escape velocity" to break away from earth's gravitational pull upon the mind. And at last came the soaring realization: *You are a part of earth—and yet, you are out among the stars.*

As we roamed the skies that night, somewhere out in the far lonesome, I strayed upon a *new* constellation: four faint points of a diamond, with a highlight star close by. "Dad—I've found a diamond!" It was some time before I could lead him to it, but at last he spied it, too, and we thrilled in our discovery. In early dawn I awoke to find only the brightest stars yet visible, and my father murmured a Shakespearian line, "'Night's candles have burnt out.' Our Diamond's been put away."

After that discovery, whenever my father and I would travel the interstellar trails, we'd eventually journey to our "Diamond"—the final stop on our space flights. We never tried to identify our constellation on the star maps, probably because we feared to find it already discovered and named. That would be like beaching our canoe on a remote island and leaping ashore in the hope that we were the first humans to tread that ground...only to discover campfire ashes and rusty cans.

Many times, after that vain search from the moving car, I tried to rediscover "The Diamond," but without success. Strange that I had forgotten about that faint star cluster for so long. But so many things crowd in between us and the stars: a degree, a career, a family, a mortgage, the starless struggle to keep up with the Joneses. Through all the astral territories I looked for the misty trinket, and at last I gave up the search for my four lost stars.

"Tell me like it was when you were a little boy, Dad."

"Okay," I said, tossing my son onto his bed with a two-hand push shot. I told him about the maple-flanked vacant lot that was our neighborhood playing field, about the beckoning roads that led out of town to the wild places, about camp-outs with my father on Iowa's Flint Creek, and in Canadian canoe country. And I told him about how I'd found, and lost, "The Diamond" constellation.

"But Dad—how could you lose a whole cons'lation?"

"Well, it's just that there are so many stars, and maybe my eyes aren't what they used to be." I patted his blond crew-cut. All the temper-trying stuff in a little scamp has vanished when he's tucked in for the night. "Say, how's about us camping out? No tent. Right under the stars!"

"Gee—swell! When?"

We drove out along the Eau Claire River to a high knoll. We'd have a good sweep of sky. You have to be choosy in selecting a launch pad. Camping wasn't quite like I remembered it. The steak was tougher, the night air more penetrating, the ground much harder! But the majestic face of night was the same. "You're still as star-struck as you ever were," I said to myself as the old wonder and awe returned.

"I see the big buttercup, Dad."

"You mean the Big Dipper?"

"Yeah, I was spoofin'." I detected his impish grin in the firelight. He hadn't yet felt the overwhelming wonder, but it would come. No use explaining or encouraging it. Like Louie Armstrong said when asked to define jazz: "Man, if you gotta ask, you'll never get to know."

I thought about my son's absorption in the TV space soaps, and how they've polluted the astral seas with shoot-'em-up violence and lust for power. Somehow, the firmament just isn't the place for the cussedness and conflict of Homo sapiens. For me, "star" has always been a sacred word—a silvery symbol with the chime of music and the power to propel us to the highest reaches of the mind. But the old myths are fading from the skies, I thought. Cygnus has lost her wings, and Sagittarius has traded in his bow on an interstellar ballistics missile. If humankind could only soar into outer space with holy awe, rather than the unholy desire to "git thar fustest with the mostest."

"Gee, Dad, there's so *many* stars!" He was breaking away from earth's gravitational pull. He was wondering if the universe stopped somewhere, or went on forever. Keep yourself sensitized to wonder, I silently pleaded. It's the power that propels us to new galaxies, new knowledge. The power that led us to the Grecian myths, the telescope, "The Big Bang."

Keep going, son, I thought. There's much to guide you: Ptolemy, Kepler, Newton, Einstein. But now, rather than pondering black holes, quarks and quasars, better you go like Jim Bridger and Kit Carson went into the great west, with wide-eyed wonder, alone. No propellant is more powerful than basic wonder, compounded by the chemistry of night and stars.

"Let's look for The Diamond, Dad."

"Okay," I said to the intense astronaut. "It's very small and dim." We searched the galactic territories. He drew me to several star groups, but we failed to find the one I'd long been seeking.

"Are you sad 'cause you lost it, Dad?"

"Oh, not really. But it'd be great to find it again." I studied the small profile alongside me. Somehow, I mused, the sight of a human face uplifted into starlight is a vision of life's peak moments. Moments such as those when lyrical fragments of the Psalms first came to David. Moments such as those when Galileo and Einstein first sensed intimations of understanding, streaming through the infinite.

It was a night charged with all the mystery of

"Ecclesiastes"—inspiring, humbling, mind-expanding, ego-shrinking. A night swept clean of vanity and vexation. A night brilliant with starlight, yet dark with the unfathomable. I thought about the stars of yesteryear, shining with assuring stability in the firmament. And about the stars of today, rushing away from us at bewildering speed, through an ever-expanding universe. I thought about the Doppler shift, the fourth dimension. And I thought about my son, wandering in awe through the cosmic places. If only he or I had been able to rediscover that distant realm with its four, faint points of silver.

"Keats Kamp" is what my father had named our site near Flint Creek, to honor his favorite poet. And as I recalled that name, one of John Keats' lines came back to sooth my frustration: *"Heard melodies are sweet, but those unheard are sweeter."*—Seen constellations are grand, but those unseen are grander, I thought. Like sculptured images on a Grecian urn, their magnificence will never fade in the light of day.

I saw in the flickering firelight that my son was asleep. Perhaps on some starry night, I thought, you'll find that elusive Diamond. But—isn't it best if it remains undiscovered? Isn't there something in the search that's better than discovery? An intensity that keeps the brain's synapses sparking; that keeps us yearning and stretching and charged with desire.

The diesel-wail of the night train sounded from far over forested hills, then tapered off southward. I glanced once more at my slumbering son, and slid down chin-deep in my sleeping bag. I took a last look at the Big Dipper, its final stars in eternal aim at Polaris. From its boundless cup there seemed to pour a radiance, for I knew that my boy had been enriched by a Diamond-bright experience. He had come to sense the overwhelming wonder. He had broken away from earth's bonds of vanity and vexation.

Floating along slumber's edge, I heard once more that

unheard melody of the spheres, whispering down our galaxy, swelling and fading like a mystical descant beyond the rhythms of the universe.

Words, too, came drifting down through the cosmos to a dying fire on a finite knoll in the infinite night, saying to me, and perhaps to the dreams of my son: *You are a part of earth—and yet, you are out among the stars.*

OF BIRDS AND BEES AND DNA

Cerulean sky, shimmering lake, rustling birches—everything pointed to a perfect family campout...until a whispered message from my spouse brought a disquieting cloud to the horizon.

We had pitched camp on a gem of a lake in Wisconsin's northern highlands. A long string of vacation days stretched sunnily ahead. I had driven the last stake for the tarp that roofed in our cooking-eating area, and was brimming with the "everything's going-our-way" feeling. Then Margaret drew near and said in deep-down serious tone, "Phil, it's high time you had a talk with Flip about the facts of life."

Back then in the 60s, kids didn't need to be informed as early as they do in today's sex-saturated, tell-it-all, show-it-all world with unsubtle, uninhibited, and unclothed Madonna-types cavorting through the mass media. Nevertheless, I knew that a frank talk with our eighth grade son was due, and I anticipated it as I do a session with the dentist's drill.

"Aw, Margaret," I replied to her verbal nudge, "let's not rush things. How about this winter?" "Now!" she said. "Take him out in the canoe and have a good, fatherly talk."

"A good, fatherly talk"—something my dad had never been able to coax himself into. Shortly before my marriage, he'd haltingly said, "Son, I should've had a discussion with you about—uh—things. But I've arranged for your older brother to take you to lunch. He'll have a good, long talk with you about—uh—things." And my big brother, ten years my senior, did a fine job. I didn't acquire much new information, but it was a sensitively executed refresher.

With a flock of unfatherly butterflies starting to swirl inside, I told Flip to grab his spinning rod and I'd paddle him to a likely fishing hole. Then the two of us shoved off for those treacherous reefs and snags that lurk in the stream of conversation about the facts of life.

I headed us into a solitary bay, thinking of those subtle, symbolic sequences that films used to segue into at the peak of a torrid love scene. Remember? Trees in orgiastic sway against a frenzied wind...clouds in passionate race before the moon...climactic crashing of waves against rockbound shores. Could I use such a symbolic approach? Alas, no escape. I had to be painfully explicit!

After a spell of aimless chatter and aimless casts toward shore, I took a deep inhalation and plunged into the subject. Straining to suppress the stutters and "ahems," I tackled the fundamentals. And I strove to include, not just the bare facts, but the higher meaning, the loftier dimension, and all that.

While I stumbled through the forbidding journey, our son sat quietly attentive in the canoe's bow. And after I'd traveled the full route from birds to bees to Homo sapiens, I lapsed into silence with the same relief I feel when clambering out of the dental chair.

Flip briefly reflected and then said, "It's all very interesting, Dad; but even more interesting, I think, is what they're discovering about the DNA molecule."

"DNA molecule?" I repeated, with what must have been a blanker than blank stare. "Yeah," he said. And then our son diverted the conversational stream from birds and bees to fruit fly experiments in genetics, and mid-1960s discoveries in biochemistry. He guided me into arcane currents of molecular research, amino acids, DNA (deoxyribonucleic acid), and the genetic code. It was a breathtaking ride!

"Where'd you learn all this?" I asked in astonishment after I'd been steered through the forty-eight human chromosomes, and the pair that determine sex. "From a science newsletter in school," Flip explained. "Real interesting stuff!"

It was an unforgettable experience, that day in our canoe on a lake in the northern highlands when I'd explained—well,

exchanged—some facts of life during "a good, fatherly talk."
And, one of these days, I'm going to brush up on that DNA
molecule thing!

GATEWAY TO SOMEWHERE

I was mowing close to a gateway that stood, sagging but defiant, just west of our barn. The tractor took an unexpected lurch, and unyielding metal crunched into decaying wood. The post fell to earth with a death groan, dragging the gate with it.

It was a painful sound, a chilling reminder of swiftly passing time—and of mortality. I swore, more in sadness than anger, switched off the ignition and sat staring at the wreckage.

It's no loss, I thought unconvincingly, my eye tracing the scarred, cross-buck pattern of the fallen gate, its rusty hinges reaching for lost moorings. But the more I studied the stricken gate, the more intense grew the pain.

I had long been aware of how useless the gateway had become. The fastening post of its other side had disintegrated long ago. So had much of the fence that had trailed on from there, leaving a gateway that closed no gap and confined no critters.

"A gateway to nowhere," I mused.

Yet I knew that aging portal still served a purpose. It preserved something of intangible value. It provided access to a beloved stretch of time. It fenced in a herd of fond memories of vibrant days when we were younger, and when the last of our brood of four was still with us.

Now that portal had been cruelly flattened.

Dismounting from the tractor, I thought back over the string of years that had slipped by since our son had measured, cut, fitted and fastened together that gateway. He had plunged into the task with an eagerness typical of the way he tackled things.

I seized the fallen gatepost, once so firm and now so spongy, and dragged it toward the brush pile. In my mind's eye, I could see the boy of yesterday, toiling with the post-hole digger, setting the uprights he had sawed from an oak he had felled, taking pains to make them perfectly vertical, then tamping in the soil. After hanging the gate, tightening its last bolt and setting the last screw, he wiped the sweat from his face and looked over his handiwork. We grinned over a handshake of happy accomplishment.

The two of us strung an electric fence around part of our wooded acreage to confine the two horses we were about to acquire. We hauled in many a station wagon load of lumber from an abandoned farmhouse, then built two stalls in the barn and laid sturdy planks over the cold concrete floor.

Through his high school years, our son frequently would saddle up and, with adventure glistening in his eyes, go cantering along the forest trails. Ah, the liveliness of those days! There was even excitement in the blended fragrance of leather, hay, grain, horse sweat and manure that permeated the barn. The horse trough was kept full, and a tank heater remained on steaming duty throughout the winter.

Charlie, a feisty Appaloosa, learned to put the bite on the heater, lifting it out of the tank and depositing it on the floor. Mornings after he pulled this trick, we'd cuss him as we swung a sledge to break the ice that had formed in the trough. But the boy soon foiled his mischievous mount by rigging up a device that held the heater firmly in place.

Those bright, brief years were spiced with the unexpected. During hunting season, spooked deer sometimes would streak through our woods, snapping fragile strands of our electric fence, inviting the horses to stray. On a night torn by icy winds, neighbors a mile away phoned to announce that our wandering pair was gallivanting around their yard.

Long and weary was the night Charlie broke out of his stall and raided the supply of rich grain-mix. After discovering Charlie's binge, we had to walk him up and down our road all through the witching hours to prevent his "foundering"—a possibly fatal result of his massive overeating.

We toughed it through a week of tension when the Appaloosa developed a severe case of snuffles. Following the vet's advice, we'd back Charlie into his stall, tie him port and starboard with his kicking legs tight against the manger so the boy could safely jab a needle into his rump, while I stood breathlessly by for moral support.

And there was the heart-stopping moment when my wife tumbled from the saddle to sprawl on the turf with one foot tangled in the stirrup. Fortunately, Pawnee stood quietly until I could free her foot. Another time our son was coaching his mother on the fine art of riding, and her violent jouncing in the saddle set her off into equally violent paroxysms of laughter, to the amusement of her coach and the bewilderment of her mount.

In his later high school days, our son became more and more caught up with trail-bike riding and less and less with equestrian rambles. Then came the bittersweet day when he departed for college. That first winter I trudged through snow and cold to continue the feeding and watering, and one of composer Jacques Brel's melancholy lines kept drifting through my mind: "All of the children vanish too soon."

Neither my wife nor I had taken wholeheartedly to horseback riding because we had great respect—no, fear—of horses. This, together with the rising cost of hay, suggested but one sensible decision. With both relief and reluctance we sold the mare—and the first night we were haunted by Charlie's mournful whinnying in the lonely darkness. Soon afterward we sold him, too, and an era of adventure came to a close.

The summer after Charlie and Pawnee trotted out of our lives, our son landed a job with the National Park Service in Montana's Glacier National Park. It was the true breakaway from home.

We saw our youngest off at the Amtrak depot in St. Paul,

toting his bulky pack down a long tunnel toward another gateway—the exit from our lives into a life of his own. We watched the distant figure pause at the tunnel's bend, turn with a final wave, then stride out of sight. For a moment we stood staring down that barren expanse, then silently clasped hands and walked away.

In the next decade our son completed college, married and pursued a teaching career in Montana mountain country. Through all those years that went galloping by, his gateway stood sturdily, comfortingly, beside the barn—and for me it evolved into a changeable symbol.

On darker days I saw it as a desolate point of departure, like that gloomy depot tunnel in St. Paul; as the exit through which our son—all four of our children—had "vanished too soon" on their eager journeys to independence. But on brighter days I saw the gateway as a port of entry through which our offspring occasionally would return in joyous reunion.

But now that treasured symbol lay rusting and rotting on the brush pile. And west of the barn, the eye could see only a stretch of lonesome space, blank and meaningless as an empty blackboard.

For quite a spell after the gateway's demise, the aching sense of loss remained. But on a recent morning when I entered the barn to fetch seed for the bird feeders, I detected a faint whiff of horse sweat and manure. And the smell of hay was unmistakably there, for I always keep a bale or so around, as much for fragrance as for mulch.

My chores completed, I stood outside the barn for a time, inhaling the crisp morning air and savoring the birds' dawn chorus. Then I stole a look at that painfully vacant place—and through the low-hanging mist I seemed to glimpse a gaunt and ghostly gateway. At least it hadn't vanished from my mind's eye.

A gateway fashioned of memory and imagination is more enduring than oak, I concluded. It withstands weather's most brutal buffeting and the weight of year piling upon year.

Then, through that wraith of a gateway, from out of the wispy trails of morning mist, a vision came into focus: sights, sounds and sensations of a memorable night of Christmas Past when we, with all four of our children, had meandered out that portal into the winter twilight with our youngest leading the mare. And while Pawnee wore no harness bells, we marched to the rhythm of Yuletide music. Snow was floating down as we chattered and chuckled, and the glory of Christmas was all around us.

I turned and walked buoyantly back to the house, my spirit aglow with the vision I had glimpsed through a ghost of a gate. And I was pondering the mystery of mental gateways, framed by both memory and anticipation—thresholds to the best of the past and brightest of the future.

Through these portals our children depart, and later return as adults, and as our most treasured friends.

Come storm, or time's relentless flow, or reckless tractor operators, there always will be a gateway out there west of our barn—a gateway to somewhere!

PERILS OF PARENTING

"If we could just get the boys interested in something—maybe sports," Margaret said. "Yeah," I replied, "we tried to get them into tennis, but that idea didn't even make it over the net."

One son was in junior high, the other in grade school, and we were a little uptight about rebellion, peer pressure, idle hands—things like that. "They need a strong interest," said Margaret, "something they'll hang with!"

Then I thought about handball. I'd loved the game ever since I was a kid. My dad had been a top-notch player, and fired me up on the game. I was a—well, pretty good player—so why couldn't I fire up my sons? I'd get them out on the court and show 'em how it's done!

The following Saturday we trotted onto the YMCA court with gloves and ball. I pep-talked them a little, trying in fatherly fashion to spark enthusiasm. I demonstrated the serve, the right and left-hand shots, the techniques of taking rebounds off side and back wall. And, with a bit of restrained pride, I showed them the "kill" shot that smacks the front wall corner a mere inch above the floor.

We started a friendly game, and soon I began to feel that something good was happening. We're bonding, I thought. But not too far into the action, an unfriendly front moved into our friendly atmosphere. The boys' enthusiasm waned as their hands stung more with each shot. Squabbles grew more heated with each body contact. After I'd broken up the third or fourth spat, I announced, striving for a patient tone, "Let's try something else. How about shooting some baskets?"

We trotted upstairs toward the gym. As fate would have it, the moment I opened the door and stepped onto the gym floor, a wildly-thrown basketball caught me smack in the nose. "You fellas go on and shoot," I gasped through pain. "I'll join you in a few minutes. Wanna get some ice for my schnozz."

With the pain numbed down somewhat, and my nose apparently still in joint, I rejoined my boys and we were soon into some frolicsome passing, dribbling and shooting. "They seem pretty enthused," I thought. "Good father-and-son stuff goin' on here." And then I went up for a rebound, was jostled in mid-air by another basket-shooter, knocked off balance, and I crashed tailbone first on the hardwood floor. "You fellas go on playing," I gasped through pain as I crawled toward the wall. "I'll join you in a few minutes. Wanna take it easy for awhile."

"You okay, Dad?" asked one son after I'd stopped seeing stars and was tottering back onto the court. "Yeah," I said, trying to sound hale and hearty while wondering whether my tailbone was crushed, or just cracked. "Let's just pass the ball around awhile until I—uh—loosen up a little."

The basketball floated around amidst our threesome for a spell, as my throbbing backside began to unparalyze a little. Soon the passes became fancier and zippier. Then someone at the other end of the floor called my name. I turned my head to look—just at the moment when one son uncorked a fast one, and the ball zoomed right into my—well, into where a guy should *never* be clobbered by a speeding basketball! "You fellas go on playing," I gasped through pain as I crawled once more toward the sidelines, accompanied by a dazed sense of deja vu. "Wanna take some time to—uh—get my wind back."

"You okay, Dad?" came the familiar question later on, when I was finally struggling to my feet. "Yeah," I said in unhale and unhearty tone, "but let's head for the showers."

When we returned home, the two boys zipped into the house, and I shuffled along in their wake. "Looks like they enjoyed it," said Margaret, absorbed in the boys' high spirits and not yet aware of my perilous condition. "Why not call the Y now and reserve a court for next week?"

"Call the Y? Reserve a court?" I gasped through pain, hobbling toward the sofa. "Call the doc! Reserve a hospital bed! I wanna get x-rayed!"

VOICES FROM DOWNSTREAM

"Something hidden; go and find it!"—That stirring command from a Kipling poem echoed through my mind the moment we sighted the weather-scarred sign, *Point Pleasant Campground*. Excitement mounted, even though I knew we wouldn't find what we were seeking. It was too elusive. Irretrievable.

We were following a not-too-accurate memory-map along a Montana road paralleling the Swan River, which flows northward along the Mission Mountain range. *The Swan!* It streams through some of the fondest territory of our past, riffling along the edges of our consciousness.

We exchanged subdued smiles as we took the familiar turnoff and headed up through towering, moss-draped larches. At the crest, we crossed faint traces of an old logging road, then coasted down toward the campsite along the Swan.

A quarter of a century before, with tent-trailer in tow and our two small sons jostling in the back seat, we had bumped over that road, tense in our eagerness to find a camping spot before dark. We had earlier tried in vain for a vacant site further north on Swan Lake. Then we had luckily discovered Point Pleasant. Only a few campers were strung along the shore and there was an open site—a choice one on the intriguing edge of wilderness.

We had found it far more than pleasant, that lofty point beside a mountain stream. Too primitive, perhaps, for the fastidious. No pump (you could fetch water at Ingram's store a few miles up the road). No convenient fireplaces with grates. No handy stack of firewood. And restrooms? Well, there were three, precariously tilting, doorless structures, not one of which was visibly designated for either *"Men"* or *"Women"*.

But its primitiveness gave Point Pleasant its unique charm.

It was verdantly wild and quiet, except for the background murmur of the Swan. Its air was brisk. Its sky was awash with that singularly western shade of bluer-than-blue.

Most of all, there was the river. From upstream it curved mysteriously into view, winding around a massive bluff. Downstream it curved mysteriously out of view, taking a westerly turn toward the peaks of the Mission range.

There is something hypnotic about a river. Its flow seems everlasting, yet tenuous. Its liquid glide soothes the mind, yet stirs thoughts on the imponderable. Its music lifts the spirit, yet whispers solemnly of time sweeping by. Its current scours out dusty channels of the mind and sends new thought-streams coursing through.—Threads of the miraculous are discernible throughout nature's fabric, but they are most visibly interwoven with the strands of moving water.

Our rediscovery plunged us into a nostalgic mood. We were surprised to find the site uninhabited. We had our pick of spots—but then we were not camping on this sentimental journey. The place seemed as sylvan and serene as we remembered it—but now the shadows were imbued with intimations of loneliness. Undertones in the atmosphere reminded us of something bright and joyous that once was here, and now was gone.

As we approached our old site, we felt a twinge on finding the same weather-beaten table, the same flame-blackened stones in the fire ring, the same scar from a lightning strike snaking down the trunk of an ancient larch, and the same spruce whose boughs had spread a second roof over our canvas one.

Looking down the slope toward the river, we half expected to see our boys emerge dripping from the stream and trot expectantly up the bank toward us and lunch. In their splashing frolic they had discovered a deep hole scooped out by the current, and they found endless delight in wading upstream, then riding the flow back down and over the awesome brink into what they called the "bathtub." We now discovered that the main current had shifted westward, leaving the "bathtub" high and dry—another reminder that cherished things are forever vanishing; that from upstream the unknown is forever flowing our way.

We spread a picnic lunch on the crude table that had been, for a fleeting interlude, the center of our family life. As we munched, we shook off our nostalgia by reliving the "bear scare." A camping neighbor had told us he had seen a black bear sow and cub the previous dusk, skulking through the underbrush. In the dead of the next night, we'd been jarred awake by a thump that set the trailer to shuddering. Our hearts were jolted into high, then superhigh at the sound of a moan *inside* our canvas home. I grabbed hatchet and flashlight, and we soon discovered to our relief that our oldest boy had fallen out of his sleeping bag and down into the well between bunks, where he lay dazed but unhurt.

We chuckled, too, over the "outhouse incident." Our first day at the Point, we had discussed with other campers the doorless and unlabeled restrooms with their high risk of indecent exposure. We all agreed upon a system for eliminating the danger. Every outhouse-user was to whistle a warning tune throughout occupancy. As double precaution, everyone approaching an outhouse was also to whistle a warning, "Here I come."

On her first venture toward one of the single-holers, Margaret, faithful to the plan, whistled merrily every step of her way. Alas, as she rounded the blind corner of the structure, her whistle terminated in a shriek when she confronted a male crouched on the splintery seat, also whistling merrily. Each whistler had drowned out the other. Our flawed plan had brought disaster!

We fondly recalled our series of evening campfires, blazing

reassuringly in the dark. Ponderosa makes leaping flames to seize the imagination. The four of us, clustered around the cordial light, had chattered away and listened to the night music of the river, punctuated by mysterious rustlings in the shadows. As part of the campfire ritual, Margaret had read selections from Mark Twain, Conrad Richter and Hal Borland. The boys listened, eyes shining in the dancing light, more deeply absorbed than they'd ever been in television's "Gunsmoke" or "Rawhide."

One morning as the boys and I were having a rock-skipping contest along the slick where the stream ran smooth and free, they urged a canoe jaunt. I'd been warned about stretches of medium-tough whitewater, but the boys' persistence won out. We drove seven miles downstream to discover a bridge where Margaret could meet us with the car. Back at camp we stashed food, jackets, and insect repellent in a canoe bag, lashed it to the center thwart, and the three of us pushed off.

The floating was easy and exhilarating. Further along we encountered riffles of mildly fast water that brought thrills unmarred by anxiety. We then encountered faster but still friendly rapids, and occasionally I felt gnawing indecision when the channel forked.

We glided around a sharp S-curve and were shocked to find ourselves drifting into a chaotic logjam. A hopeless impasse—but then we thought of Margaret, waiting for us downstream. So we slogged and splashed and shoved and tugged, threading our canoe over, under and around the jumble, finally struggling through to open water.

Gliding freely again, we rejoiced and I lit a fresh cigar. Minutes later, from around the next bend came an ominous roar of rushing water. Soon we were plunging down a frothy raceway—and there at a sharp bend, waiting in ambush, was a huge, half-submerged snag, its branches jabbing out in all directions. "Hard on the right!" I screamed to Flip in the bow as I paddled desperately to steer us clear. But the current sucked us smack into the monstrous snag, and in an instant we were under water with the capsized canoe above us. We thrashed frantically to avoid being trapped in the tangle of underwater branches. Luckily, the three of us fought free and shot to the surface alongside our overturned craft, gasping in relief. We sputtered and joked as we drifted into quiet water, but our laughter was under-girded with a solemn thankfulness.

When we were again floating free and easy on a benign current, jubilant and water-soaked, Randy glanced back at me, chuckled and said: "Betcha that's one you'll never finish, Dad." I then realized that I was still clenching a soggy cigar between my teeth.—Days later, Swan River was still in my sinuses; months later, droplets of it were still under my watch crystal.

And now, twenty-five years later, the Swan's waters still sparkled—will forever sparkle—in our memories. We two lingered at the table, reminiscing over the time the four of us had spent in this enchanting place. We thought about our small boys then and our mature sons now, traveling different mainstreams of marriage and career. We thought, too, about our daughters, the two oldest of our brood, with whom we'd also shared many a rollicking adventure at both camp site and home site. What experiences the six of us had shared: joys, sorrows, raptures, fears, highs, lows, smooth water, rough water. How could they all have drifted away so soon on life's capricious currents, to such far-scattered destinations!

We gathered up the lunch remnants and, hand-in-hand, returned to our car. We paused there for a last panoramic view of Point Pleasant on the Swan, wondering if we would ever come this way again. Yet, even if we never returned, we knew that this sanctuary would continue to renew and enrich us.

We climbed into the car and headed back toward the blacktopped world. At the crest of the hill, I paused and rolled the window down. The conifers soughed in a transient breeze. A crow's raucous cry shrilled overhead and faded off down toward the river. In the hush that followed, drifting up to us through the solitude, from years and years downstream, came phantom echoes of boyish laughter.

VOICES FROM

THE WILD PLACES

TENTING ON THE OLD CAMPGROUND

We stood in the shoreline shadows, watching the play of moonlight upon the lake, listening to melodic strains of silence that you never hear in town. "There's nothing better'n camping," said my son, sidling closer to me. I squeezed his shoulder in silent agreement.

We turned from the silvery scene to study our camp, a few paces off through the spruce and birches. Under the gas lantern with its reassuring hiss of radiant energy was clustered the rest of our family. The smallest one lounged in his mother's lap, half listening to a story and half listening to voices of the forest night. The two girls were absorbed in books. Beyond them stood the tent, splashed with lantern light.

This was *home*—this bit of canvas, ropes and poles. With our six pairs of hands we had erected a roof and walls, captured a speck of wilderness atmosphere, and made it our own for a spell.

Earlier that day, things hadn't seemed quite so serene. "There's the spot for the tent," I had said on arriving, "and we can rig up the tarp right here."

The four kids simultaneously expressed four different ideas, and then wife Margaret broke in. "Here's the setup," she announced. "The tent here, the tarp over there. Then I'll have a U-shaped kitchen."

"U-shaped kitchen?" I asked.

"Sure—back the car in like so, and the trunk will be our pantry."

"Okay," I said, and was soon maneuvering the car into position as the south vertical of a U formation. Veering off the beaten track, I backed onto a rocky hummock, and our purring engine began roaring like a brash motorcycle. "There went my muffler," I shrieked. "All for a lousy U-shaped kitchen!"

But it takes more than a shattered muffler to shatter a true camper's spirit. Even rain needn't wash out optimism. Like the time on one of our first outings when low and somber clouds approached. We had a stingy tarp suspended over our table, and decided we'd better enlarge this roof. We rigged a big plastic cloth as an extension, with the help of clothespins. A drizzle began, and we settled down to read with the mist tinkling pleasantly on our canopy. We had that smug feeling of having licked the elements.

But the patter soon became a drumming downpour. Our plastic roof began to droop as pools gathered in its ever-deepening depressions. There was a sickening sound of collapse and a rivulet plunged down the back of my collar, down my pant legs, into my shoes. Several clothespins had given up, releasing an overhead reservoir.

There was laughter, but not from me. Then Kathleen screamed, "Look—our tent!" Water was flowing toward it from all directions. We now realized that most of the immediate terrain took a slight slope toward our canvas home.

I stood there, drenched in rain and futility. But the women of the family raced for trenching tools. The boys and I sloshed after them, grabbing sticks, cans, anything. We tore at the rocky, rooty soil with tools and fingernails.

"No use," I groaned. I had hacked a long trench from tent to table. Now water was burbling into the ditch and flowing uphill—apparently—toward the tent. But the girls and their mother fought on, throwing up a dike against the worst of the flood. The boys were wallowing happily in the mud puddles. Within my soggy being, a faint spark flickered anew. I grabbed a can and started to try and turn the uphill trench into a downhill one.

We later sagged to rest, and I looked in awe upon the maze of trenches that wound off in all directions. I thought solemnly about Ypres and Chateau Thierry.

By supper time, the rain had diminished to a downpour. We slurped soup and rainwater, crouching under the stingy tarp that partially protected our table but left our backsides exposed.

"Oh well, we'll have a cheery campfire tonight," Margaret said.

"Yeah?" I spluttered, glancing into the sodden underbrush. "In all my scouting days I never learned how to start a fire under water."

"Other campers have fires in rainy weather," she said.

"Then they must have some dry firewood stashed away."

"Split some logs," she suggested. "The insides are dry."

"I couldn't split a pencil with that little hatchet of ours."

We sat around a gas-lantern fire that night. "This is almost as cheery as a campfire," I said, my words sinking into the damp silence.

"Next time we camp," Margaret announced, "we'll have an ax that splits logs."

"And how!" the four kids chimed in.

"And we'll have a *big* tarp that covers *us* along with the table."

"And how!" the four voices rang out.

"And we'll pitch our tent on high ground."

"And how!" came the chorus, my voice joined with the other four.

Rain isn't the only element that can gang up on a camper. At the simmering edge of the Dakota Badlands one July afternoon, we stopped at the "Last Chance" ice house, filled everything hollow with cubes, chunks and chips, then headed into the place of fantastic formations and fantastic temperatures.

"Let's hike," urged the boys at sight of the first turnout.

"Don't you understand?" I asked, clinging to the sweat-slippery steering wheel. "We'd die out there!"

"Reeeely, Dad?" Randy asked. "How come?"

"We'd just fry until we die."

"I wanna hike!"

"Look—first we'll find the campsite. We'll pitch our tent in a nice, shady spot. Then we'll hike in the cool of the evening, or the cool of the morning, or whenever the cool happens around here."

We wound around Vampire Peak, down past the Monument headquarters, and paused on a ridge where the land sloped into a treeless plain. *"Camp Site,"* the sign said. We stared in disbelief at the vast, sunburned stretch, shimmying away in a heat-wavy dance that clearly spelled sunstroke. A few picnic tables roofed by wooden canopies formed pitiful dots of shade. "That can't be the campsite!" Margaret's words shrivelled away in the furnacy air.

"Must be," I said. "See—there's a spot near each table to pitch a tent."

We circled the area, our spirits falling, our car's temperature gauge rising. We returned to the air conditioned headquarters building. "Is that the main campsite?" I inquired of a cool lady at the information desk, and I described the Sahara-like scene.

"Yes. What seems to be your problem?"

"Well, we were sorta hoping for a few trees, and—you know—a bit of shade."

"Oh? There's another site twenty miles on, with a few cottonwoods."

"Great!" I brightened, already sensing the cool rustle of leaves.

"But its strictly primitive. There's no water there." The refreshing rustle of leaves evaporated like a mirage, and we drove somberly back to Death Valley. We pitched camp in a wobbly, slow-motion way, making for the water faucet every few minutes.

But dusk finally came in a cooling—well, somewhat cooling—march across that grotesque landscape, and a constant breeze drifted through our tent that night. We arose before daybreak, breakfasted, and broke camp. Then we roamed the trails through those eerie, pasteled canyons while they were awash with the slanting rays of sunrise. We were glad we had camped in the Badlands.

Later, as we sped west, we passed the primitive campsite and I saw a puny row of cottonwood shrubs. They would have cast as much shade as a row of fence posts. They weren't even big enough to rustle!

A camping family takes the rain, the heat, whatever comes, and makes the best of it. There are no thermostats to regulate the environment, no faucets for turning off the rain showers, no push buttons, no servicemen at the other end of a telephone—and *no telephone!* You escape from all the gadgetry, and learn that you can get along without it. And when you return to the other world, you appreciate the gadgetry as you never did before.

In camping, your family's comfort and protection depend upon your own two hands—upon the skill with which you pitch a tent, sling a tarp, secure your shelter with taut ropes and firm knots.

"What's that knot, Dad?" asked Flip, when we were setting up camp in the Black Hills.

"Lumberman's hitch," I said, with the brisk tone of a seasoned outdoorsman.

"What knots do you use for the clothesline?" asked daughter Chris.

"Lumberman's hitch."

"What about the ropes for the tarp?" Kathleen inquired.

"Lumberman's hitch."

"What about when you tie the ridge pole on top of the car?" asked Randy.

"Lumberman's hitch."

"Gee, Dad," Flip said, "a lumberman's hitch must be a reeeely good knot."

"Well, it's the only—it's one I remember from my scouting days. Easy to tie and untie. Seems to hold real well."

"Do you *ever* tie other knots?" Kathleen asked.

"Oh sure," I said, "for shoestrings, and—uh—we'd better hurry along. There's lots more to be done."

There is deep satisfaction in the plain and simple work that's a part of the camping life. Your mind becomes unhitched from its routine harness and is free to roam lush pastures when you plunge into such elemental stuff as erecting a shelter, splitting wood, building a fire...and tying lumberman's hitches.

I lay awake one camping night on my cushion of air, studying the star-powdered sky through the tent window, and listening to the tender breath of those around me. I thought about the other home we six shared—the sturdy, 50-weeks-a-year one, crammed with comforts and joys and liveliness. But, I thought, there are little magnets scattered throughout that home which tend to pull us off in separate directions: the separate rooms, the walls, the terrible T's of television and telephone and other divisive things and forces.

There are no such magnets in a camping home, I concluded; nothing to fragment a family. A tent is one, all-embracing room, and it holds a precious closeness within its fragile walls—and at that moment, Randy's close elbow jabbed my ear as he tossed in his sleep. Later, from the other side, Chris' close knee brushed along my ribs. There is bruisingly real togetherness in family camping.

Best of all in the camping life is dawn. Under a canvas roof, one isn't isolated from the best colors, the best sounds, the best sensations of existence. The world comes rustling, pattering, singing, buzzing, murmuring, shining to life. One by one the children surface to wakefulness, sink again to slumber, surface once more, raise tousled heads, then wriggle to their feet in a magic room that is exceedingly receptive to the dawn's fresh promise.

Tenting is only a fleeting existence, but it brings permanent values to a family. You submerge yourselves in the wide-open spaces. You pad along for a week or two on resilient pine needles and the wind-strewn leaves of last year's summer. You roam carefree over hills, through valleys, along shores, and you find a rare exhilaration.

It is a rather somber hour when you break camp, and the wilds seem to close in, reclaiming the niche that was once your family possession. You take a last look at the spot where your home so swiftly dissolved, and you see only lonesome space. A chipmunk darts-pauses-darts across your former living room. A chickadee whirls down to seek crumbs on your deserted table. The familiar clump of trees, bereft of your tent and tarp, have lost their intimacy, and now blend with the impersonal forest. The fire ring, where you laughed and chattered and sang to the orange dance of flame, is ash-grey and lifeless.

You drive away with a twinge of pain, but with a spark of pride, too. For you had joined hands here to tame a bit of wilderness, capture some of its magic and hold it within your family circle for a spell. And you know that some of its pungency, its freshness, its silence, its sunlight, its strength, is returning with you to the more enduring home.

"NOW IS THE WINTER OF OUR DISCONTENT..."

Though many a fine Shakespearian line lingers fondly in my mind, that opener for *"Richard the Third"* is nettlesome, because I am more contented than discontented with winter. The "incomparable bard" goes on to contrast winter with "glorious summer." But I find the frigid season fully as glorious—zesty, sparkling, invigorating, after a summery stretch of languor.

We who desire not to flee southward when autumn fades see the shivery side of the calendar as our "character-building" time. Oh sure, there are interludes of winter discontent: damp and gloomy days...times when the temperature dips drastically low, or the wind penetrates drastically deep...mornings when we discover that the cold has paralyzed the car battery, or the uncaring snowplow has heaved up a windrow that barricades us from the world. Yet, there's something in wading unflinchingly into icy blasts, overwhelming drifts, and a minus-50-degree chill factor that brings a warming triumph, strengthens us, builds character!

One writer I know had this to say about the Wisconsin climate: *"Robins sometimes winter here...but they worry a lot."*

We unfeathered humans worry, too: "What if the oil burner fizzles out?" "What if there's a power outage?" "What if the water pipes freeze and burst?" But such worries help us fight boredom and complacency, keep us on our chilblained toes, lead us to the spirit-warming conviction expressed by that same "incomparable bard": *"How sweet are the uses of adversity!"*

My wife and I toughed it through a 40-below adversity, our second winter in north-central Wisconsin (1947). We were then renting a drafty house with a temperamental furnace, and the best I could do was get the inside temperature up to a luke-cold 50 degrees. There were few "sweet uses" to be found in the adversity—but we survived.

Our first winter after moving out in the woods, a remarkably cold night closed in on us—but it was cloudless and windless with a full moon. "Dad, let's take a snowshoe hike," suggested our adventurous son, Randy. "But Rand, it's way below zero. We'd die out there!" was my enthusiastic reaction. But soon our undaunted son had me plodding unwillingly into bone-chilling adversity. Our insulated underwear, sorrels, and goose-down served us magnificently, so from 10 P.M. to near-midnight we snowshoed through bracing air and commanding quiet, transversing crisp shadows laid out by a blazing moon. What a magical time, under a thousand gleaming stars—"sweet uses" to be found only in winter's adversity.

When I step out to tend the bird feeders on a still, subzero dawn with the sunlight glistening along each snow-powdered pine, spruce and oak limb, an inner glory is ignited that cannot be sensed at any other point around the calendar.

Another "sweet use of adversity" is slipping into "skinny skis" and gliding off along the river and through the woods, seemingly soaring just above a fresh and pure white snowfall. And what care we that the temp is hovering just a shiver or two above zero! We float along through a silent and brilliantly shining world that is only to be discovered in the cold-yet-warm heart of wintertime. Ah—our character-building season! Our spirit-building season! The Winter of our Content!

Come February, we will saddle up our maroon Buick and gallop off to the southwest for some Elderhosteling and exploring. But, mind you, we will *not* be seeking to escape the shivery depth of Wisconsin's winter. Rather, we'll be looking for an intellectual warming, and it's mere coincidence that our chosen Elderhostel is scheduled for the cold side of the calendar. Honest!

Late February will have us back in the invigorating north, digging into the aftermath of yet another blizzard, seeking a snow shovelful of "sweet uses" in a heap of "adversity."

ROAMING THE SUNDOWN TERRITORY

Excitement kicks up inside of me whenever we head out on a trip—and the "vibes" are the strongest when the dashboard compass reads "West." Perhaps it's because of my early reading of Zane Grey, or later reading of DeVoto and Stegner. Or it might be due to the herd of western films that galloped across the screens of my childhood. Whatever the cause, the sundown territory has always had more magnetic pull than does any other point of the compass. For me, it always has been, always will be, the *Great* West!

Fondest of all my "sundown" memories are those stemming from a tent-trailer safari with our children when they were at a tender age. We headed west, and the first high point on that journey, both physically and mentally, was reached when we ascended from the Great Plains into the foothills of the front range in Colorado—a transition from the amazing horizontals to the amazing verticals of western territory.

Long before the spectacular "verticals" loomed along the skyline, we had seen garish signs along the way, announcing that "this is the place where the West begins." But such signs must be viewed with skepticism, for the Great West is mainly a state of mind. It begins to form and build within your consciousness somewhere out along the gentle swells of the great plains, when you first sense that you are becoming submerged in vast distances, with the faint blue, far-off horizon beckoning you on westward.

You also find yourself encountering distinctly western highway signs: "Caution—Dangerous Crosswinds"..."Open Range"..."Danger—Drifting Sand." So, it's a combination of specific road signs, and abstract signs spelled out by the landscape, and invisible signs flashing a wordless message across your mental screen, announcing that you have pushed beyond that mysterious and elusive place "where the West begins."

When you are westering, you are confronted by startling contrasts: prairies stretching out toward forever, and violently upthrusting mountain ranges...endless tablelands, and strangely tilted buttes and mesas...expanses of grasslands and expanses of desert tinted with bluish sage and amber heat-haze...barren treelessness and towering masses of spruce and orange-barked ponderosa.

Having visited the Grand Canyon's southern rim on a previous trip, we opted for the north rim on this expedition. Which is more impressive? It's like Hamlet versus Macbeth. But as campers, we prefer the north rim because it thrusts its parapets a thousand feet higher, is far more primitive, and because the drive down from Jacob's Lake winds through a serenely beautiful stretch of forest and mountain meadows. And there's the awesome view from Bright Angel Point, where the purple distances fall away from three sides!

We reached Lake Mead at sunset on a Saturday and had to settle for "overflow area." But we landed a pleasant site, bordered by lush desert flowers, and pitched camp in the cool of the evening. We took a dip in the lake at dusk, then returned to our camp after dark, making the discovery that one sees a thousand more stars blazing in desert skies.

Some landscapes are to be tasted, some to be chewed, and some to be thoroughly digested. Our national and state parks are in the latter category, and the only way to digest them is to climb out of your car and take to the trails. We followed unforgettable paths in Bryce, Zion and Grand Canyon Parks, and experienced immeasurably more than can be gained from a moving car. We stored away a host of magnificent visions —and beneficial results also showed up in our leg muscles, our lungs, our appetites, and in deep slumber after the darkness won out over our finite firelight.

Our westering finally ended on the Pacific Coast, and we

turned northward up the famous Cabrillo Highway—the most spectacular road we had ever traveled. The rugged coastal range, and golden hills with vivid-green live oaks and cedars, the looping road with its dramatic upsweeps, downsweeps and sidesweeps, all continue to flash through our minds.

And unforgettable sounds still ring upon the inner ear: the rhythmic swish of the surf at the great dunes near Carmel, where the sand is volcanic grey and the cliffs rise sheer and tumultuous...the challenging scream of an eagle, gliding eye-level with us as we climbed to the top of the world at Big Sur.

We discovered a spot to match a camper's fondest dream at California's Big Basin State Park north of Santa Cruz. Generously spaced sites are sprinkled among majestic redwoods—and alluring hiking trails fan out in all directions. A climb to Ocean View Summit brought us a glimpse of the Pacific forty miles westward.

Turning back at last in an easterly direction, we traveled to Twin Falls, Idaho, where we followed the Snake River upstream across irrigated farmlands, finally reaching the deep mountain valley that John Colter wandered into, wide-eyed, more than a century ago, after he left the Lewis and Clark Expedition. We camped high on a ridge above the river, where a mountain range rears upward from the opposite bank. We immediately came to know the Snake as "a river in a hurry!"

We camped for an enjoyable spell on our ridge, with a generous spread of pines and alpine flowers around us, and with the river whispering incessantly from far below. We left the Jackson Hole country with reluctance—and traveling with us as a permanent companion was the memory of the Tetons, ascending toward the stratosphere from that great, lush valley with a restless river curving through it.

We headed homeward via the boundless variety of Yellowstone Park, then crested the Wyoming Big Horns through Powder River Pass, and tasted our final mountain experience at the ponderosa-strewn Black Hills. We arrived home with 8,000 more miles on our odometer. Our faces were brown. Our legs were stronger, and so were our lungs. We had roamed through the sundown wind, sun, and mountain air. We had wandered through sage, sand, and the lavender lupine of high meadows. We had absorbed a long line of sparkling scenes which, "recollected in tranquility," as Wordsworth observed, have continued to enrich and refresh us through all the intervening years.

Camping, of course, is not all idyllic. There are expected and unexpected discomforts—and, at times, "discomfort" is too mild a word! There are bugs, cold, heat, rain, wind, physical and mental irritations. There are times when even seasoned campers curse themselves for leaving creature comforts so far behind—but later on they come to laugh off the not-so-sunny side of the camping life.

The most comic happenings, the most stirring scenes, the most cheering fires under frosty stars will be remembered and talked about when we are grandparents, and when our children are parents. Breathless moments of discovery and awe will continue to rush over us like the eternal Pacific surf at Half Moon Bay.—The final camp must be broken...but then you never completely break camp; it remains pitched in your mind forever.

Campers are some of the finest people you will ever meet. They are temporarily removed from the struggle for status and the almighty dollar. You find them in the midst of being themselves. They have taken time out to savor their world. Every now and then you see them caught up in religious awe at a dramatic overlook, overwhelmed by the wonder and majesty spread out to the vanishing point.

In family camping there is a necessity for closeness, cooperative effort, and the rapid ironing out of frictions.

There is a sense of exploring together, discovering together, that brings you home feeling closer, more in harmony, and more aware of the miracles of existence.

And there is a deep feeling of renewal. You have been submerged for a time in humbling vastness, in pure wildness, in the freshness and fragrance of the natural world. Irritations and concerns have dissolved away in prairie wind, in misty distances, in unattainable heights and purple depths.

On the bank of the "River in a Hurry" in northwest Wyoming, where John Colter and Jim Bridger once roamed, we built a final campfire the night before we bid farewell to the Teton range. We studied the leaping and twisting flames, and the star fire gleaming through the pine boughs. We listened to the soft play of night sounds. The moon blazed above the mountains, standing proud and lonely across the river, flooding their slopes in silver and shadow.

In silence we watched the fire fade down to embers, slowly surrendering to all-enveloping darkness. Yet, that fire flares on boldly in the mind's eye, warming us through cold and bitter times, illuminating the grey gloom that sometimes steals in, bringing us again and again the glowing revelations that await the explorer of the Sundown Territory.

THE TRAIL TO SANCTUARY

Our ski trail starts just beyond our doorstep, meandering through the woods and along the river, and we're on intimate terms with every inch of it.

At the foot of a gentle slope in a cluster of white pines, we glide through Deer-Run-Interchange. Further on, we curve around Dutchman's-Breeches-Bend, where we know that later, in the après-ski season, a host of white pantaloons will be fluttering in the spring breeze. Cruising by Fox-Den-Point, we often find a sprinkling of sandy soil on the snow, like a smidgen of cinnamon on whipped cream. At Slough Crossing we maneuver carefully on a purple wax day to avoid an icy coating on our skis.

When the wind begins stripping away autumn's colors, we venture out with chain saw and pruning shears to cut away obstructing windfalls, snip off intruding branches, and uproot saplings that had the temerity to sprout within our glide-way. Then we keep a weather eye on the horizon, hoping for an early blitz from Canada.

When sufficient snow powders the land, we launch into the season's first trail-breaking—a joyful ceremony! We plop-plop along like trudging snowshoers, spurred on by the thought of our next tour when we'll be gliding instead of plodding. We occasionally pause for a backward glance at our wake across the white stretches—a slender, dual track undulating over slope and swale, winding through sheltering oak and pine and birch. Nearly as exhilarating as a rhythmical stride-and-glide is the look of our trail, clean-cut and as unobtrusive as a whisper in wilderness solitude.

The cross-country skier's world is compounded of snow and stillness: snow broken only by a duet of sharply-etched lines; stillness broken only by the soft swish of skis and muted plunk of poles.

By our second or third tour, we find signs of invasion upon our ski-way: delicate impressions left by mice and squirrels, the bolder imprint of rabbit and fox, and the deep, split-curve mark of deer. This graceful tracery is the language used by the natural world in communicating with us, and we read it eagerly.

Sooner or later, though, we find a far more strident language imprinted on our trail—raucous signs that a snowmobiler or ATV rider has invaded our hallowed ground. Even though we know it's eventually bound to happen, the discovery still shocks us. The ski-way we have fondly tended has been rubbed out by a mechanized rider—one who travels too fast to glimpse Deer-Run-Interchange or Fox-Den-Point; one who, when whirling around Dutchman's-Breeches-Bend, sees no vision of springtime beauty to come.

The unique ambience of our trail has vanished. The beckoning way is now a beaten way. The solitude has lost its soothing spell. There is now something alien in our intimate strip of terrain. Here there was once a sanctuary; now it is gone.

It is disturbing to realize that something you cherish, something you create and nourish with pride and care, can be instantly obliterated. Our once slender glide-way that had been as modest as a whisper in the wintry stillness is now a waffled path, blatant as a bellow in the midst of silent meditation. Our trail's once impressionable surface is now as unyielding as Interstate 94. It is no longer an open communication line with nature. We have been disconnected.

"Alas, the best-laid trails of mice and men..." we think as we ski onward, heavy-footed and heavy-hearted, down the churned-up highway. Bitter questions simmer in our minds: "Don't they have enough speedways of their own?" "Do they realize that in one roaring run they destroy all the results of our painstaking trail-tending?"

We strive to think positively, with our skis slipping laterally on the sloping, ice-hard surface. "We skiers must try to understand the mechanized jockey's addiction to speed and horsepower, and the lure of the road not yet taken," we tell ourselves. "But then, too, mechanized riders should try to understand the thrill of the silent glide, propelled by muscle and tendon power, through untrammeled whiteness." And one fact dominates our somber musings: When we invade their trails, they can't even tell we've been there; when they invade our trails, they annihilate them!

We recently skied forth on a clear morning into new snow, with the temperature a few shivers above zero—pale green wax weather. The trail beckoned, showing no trace of snowmobile or ATV upon the fresh powder. We poled-and-stroked along under a brilliant blue sky, gliding in and out of the shadows that dappled our ski-way, with snow-decked pines all around us gleaming in the sun.

"They haven't been here yet," I exulted as we drifted along weightlessly. When we zoomed down a long slope through the radiant atmosphere, joy came rushing through us, intermingled with frosty air. All earthly cares streamed from our minds to vanish in our wake. We savored the sensation of ascending while descending. We double-poled in cadence with the rhythms of elation pulsing through us, and in our acceleration we seemed to rise on winged skis to a higher level of being, soaring along just above the slender track that led us on and on through unblemished whiteness and stillness.

When weather, mood and circumstances are right, the cross-country skier sometimes enters a mystical world—a sanctuary far away from all regrets about yesterday, all anxieties about tomorrow; far away from all gnawing expectations of unseasonable thaw, or freezing rain, or mutilating invasion of the trail.

It is only a momentary sanctuary—but it is a wonderful place, and the way there begins just beyond our doorstep.

THE MORNING SHOW

"Margaret, look! They're back together again. Maybe they've been to a marriage counselor!"

My excitement had been ignited, not by a TV soap, but by a scene beyond our window of a pair of cardinals at our feeder. For a long spell, only the male had shown up for our offering of sunflower seed—a lonely flash of crimson in the dawn. Had the female "needed more space"? Had the male found a more "significant other"? Were there irreconcilable differences? Had a hawk zoomed in to leave a solitary mate? Now the questioning was over.

Our early mornings center upon warmup exercises, breakfast, and the feathery show outside our windows. The cardinals are the protagonists—the regal male, darting in with his striking black mask, and the more subtly-hued female, making her modest entrance.

But the mainstay players are the chickadees, whirring in to snatch a seed, then whirring out to crack the hull on a birch limb. These consistent performers are momentarily upstaged when a nuthatch scampers headfirst down a pine trunk; or a raucous bluejay plunges onto center stage to strut his blue-and-white stuff; or a woodpecker flits in to the suet basket, rears back its head, and poises for vigorous attack. What variety of song, plumage, and flowing action in the morning show!

How well I remember a bird that played a major role in my boyhood. I had made a slingshot and sharpened my aim through long practice on inanimate targets. Prowling the yard one evening, weapon in hand, I decided to seek live prey. I spied a robin on an elm branch, silhouetted against the sunset. I pulled back the loaded pouch, took aim, and was about to let fly when the bird tilted its black head and poured out a trill. Something about that fragment of song instantly dissolved my ignoble intent, and I turned away to follow unlethal pursuits.

Not once in the intervening years have I taken aim at a bird or at any living thing.

Strange that a single tremolo from a robin could make a lasting impression. Yet, how ironic to know that bird song is but a territorial proclamation, according to ornithologists. Exquisite, spirit-lifting notes—but translated, they say with melodic truculence: "Keep out of my space!"

But at least our feathery species claim their territory with music, save for some types with dissonant voices. What a contrast to the ways humankind has staked claims through the ages. We've built walls; dug moats; erected barricades; strung fences; sunk missile silos; patrolled land, sea and air corridors with blustering fire power.

How different human history could be if our species were programmed to make joyful noise rather than weapons when trying to protect our turf—if it were our dominant instinct to sing our claims to continents—if we were compelled to create harmonious sound rather than intercontinental ballistic missiles and other ingenious forms of "mutually assured destruction"!

Perhaps there's a bit of wisdom to be learned from denizens of the warbling world. True, their life is rigidly programmed by instinct rather than reason, and it's a day-to-day fight for survival. Yet, there's a flowing, soaring, ethereal dimension visible and audible in the world of the airborne.

So we stay tuned to the morning show—to the continuing serial at cereal time. Many, no doubt, prefer the suspenseful "Who-Dunnit?" on the TV screen, but our favorite, by far, is the "Who-Sung-It?"—the even more intriguing question raised by joyful notes heard just beyond our window screen.

"MAKING A LITTLE DIFFERENCE..."

I was racing against the clock—against the threat of being overtaken by a rush of early snow and deep frost. My muscles yearned for rest. My fingers yearned for warmth. My nose yearned for Kleenex.

We'd just learned that the timbered tract south of us was on the market. We cherish our sylvan seclusion, which explains our favorite saying: "Happiness is never having to draw our drapes." So an urgent objective was resounding in my mind: *"Plant a Border-Screen of Pines."* And the time was *now*, before a sharp frost turned the ground granite-hard.

A multitude of young Norway pines thrive throughout our acreage, but I determined to be extremely selective, recalling the story about the old gent who trudged up to the checkout with a bottle of wine. "Sir," said the clerk, "that brand's on special if you buy a case." "Young lady," the oldster said, "at my age I don't even buy green bananas!"

"At my age," I said to myself, traipsing with readied shovel into our woods, "I don't even plant short trees." I'd dig out only five-to-six footers. That meant a large and heavy root-ball to hoist into the cart, but it'd be worth it.

Conditions were perfect: dormant trees, moist soil that held together well, invigorating air. So I dug, hoisted, hauled, cleared competing brush, dug again, planted, watered, added enriched soil, tamped, straightened, tamped again, watered again, added peat moss, and set off for another choice Norway.

All through the day I repeated that routine. Next morn, after a deep and dreamless sleep, I plunged into the task again, spurred by a lower temperature. And the next day. And the next, with the cold ominously intensifying.

At last, with snowflakes starting to whirl down and frigid air stiffening the soil, I tamped in the last pine—Norway Number Fifty-Seven. My bosky border was complete, from road to river.   A *living* boundary to preserve our sylvan sanctuary. I wearily tramped the entire line for a recount. Yup—fifty-seven! I hauled my lame lumbar to the house with a triumphant glow mollifying my aches and twinges.

Long after we two have rounded the final bend in our lifestream, our former sanctuary will be graced with a lofty row of red pines, crowns aspiring toward greater heights, orange-tinged trunks gleaming in sunlight, long-needled boughs swaying in soothing wind song.   Perhaps, next to four cherished offspring, that screen of verdant grandeur will be the most lasting mark we'll leave behind us—and that would be a satisfying thing.

When it comes to trees, we puny humans are a transient species.   Take the General Sherman Sequoia, earth's largest living thing, which has known life for 2500 years.   Or the western juniper in the Sierra Nevada, which has endured since about 2000 B.C.! A tree is a thing to admire, as well as to shrink the human ego. It seeks only its share of soil, water and sunlight. It lusts not for fame or fortune. It purifies rather than pollutes the atmosphere. It brings beauty and tranquility to the world.

Years ago I read an unforgettable line in *American Forests* magazine. It described a retired forester out on his land in somber and hostile weather, kneeling down upon the earth to plant seedlings…"trying to make a little difference on this side of forever."

In our remaining years, we will come to sense the full meaning in that phrase—and also in poet John Keats' line: *"A thing of beauty is a joy forever."* We will have the pleasure of watching our ever-green, ever-growing border along our sanctuary, multiplying its luxuriant needle clusters; of hearing our tall sentinels sing softly in the wind; of seeing their boughs becoming more and more intimately intertwined. We'll marvel as a myriad of cone miracles appear, and as lithe, orange-brown trunks grow ever more sturdy. Now and then we'll exchange smiles as we say: "Happiness is never having to draw our drapes."

And perhaps we'll also come to say, with more humility than pride: "Maybe, for at least a blink of time, '...we've made a little difference on this side of forever.'"

"SO YOU'RE COMING INSIDE THE STOCKADE..."

...said a long-time friend, on learning about our agonizing decision to move into Wausau from our forested acreage on the Wisconsin River.   "Inside the Stockade"—those words conveyed an upbeat meaning that continued to bolster us through all the turmoil and pain of preparing to relocate.

We were sure, until recently, that we'd spend all our remaining days "outside the stockade."   "They'll carry me out of here feet first," I always said.   But the passing years bring changes, and after almost three decades in our wild place, I'll be moving out on my own two feet, under my own power.   A tough but wise decision, and my spouse and I are thankful that we're making this late-stage journey into "civilization" TOGETHER!

When we settled in the woods, the youngest of our offspring was still with us, and what adventures we three shared: rewiring, remodeling, reroofing...installing thermopane windows...drilling a new well...replacing a primitive septic system for an up-to-code one...adding a family room with a California driftwood stone fireplace...fixing up the barn and stringing electric fence to take on two horses...felling, pruning, planting, and transplanting trees...carving out a third-of-a-mile ski trail along the river and through our woods.

Our sylvan surroundings brought us pleasure that never diminished.   With each dawning I'd gaze outside and repeat a Robert Frost line: "Whose woods these are, I think I know..." And we shared a saying of our own: "Happiness is never having to close your drapes."

Each year's highlight was at Christmas, when all our offspring came from far-scattered places for reunion at "The Ranch."   We roamed our woods together, skied our trail, chattered and laughed, feasted and reminisced, and joined in silent communication when meditating over the luminous, leaping play of flames upon our hearth.

So, why are we shifting from "The Ranch" to a ranch house in town? Well, we aren't quite as rugged as we once were, though we expect to keep biking, hiking, skiing, and swimming well into our eighth decade. Then, too, our frequent trips into Wausau seem longer and longer, especially in winter when the road is often treacherous. And, of late, we find ourselves thinking: "What if good health does a fast fade? What if disability sneaks up? What about the inevitable time when one of us is left alone?" Such are the disturbing "What if's" that invade the mind in wakeful night hours when you dwell "outside the stockade" and you're nearing eighty.

We'll be revising that line by Robert Frost: "Whose woods those were, I think I know..." But there are some good-sized Norway pines around our future Wausau place, and some spruce. And I'll be planting a birch clump or two, and some junipers. By city standards, our lot is fair-sized. (Something within me demands a yard to putter around in, "until they carry me away feet first".)

We're sure we can lure a melodious assortment of birds to our feeders. There's a fireplace for the heap of oak that I've split and stashed away. And most importantly, we'll have ample room for future gatherings of our clan.

Yet, what a mix of feelings as we prepare to pull up stakes: sorting through things; hauling stuff to Goodwill, Habitat for Humanity, and the county landfill; reducing useless things to ashes in blazing fires behind the barn.

Can we actually leave "The Ranch"? The soothing solitude? The swings, trapeze and sandbox where our grandchildren frolicked? The badminton/croquet/volleyball court west of the barn? The split rail fence meandering westerly and southerly? The horseshoe court in the shade of the monarch oak? The plot under the sheltering white pine where our two dogs are buried? The barn where, on dampish days, we still catch a faint whiff of hay and horse sweat? The screened porch where we breakfasted in morning sunlight and lounged on summer evenings, listening to rustling night sounds? The northeast corner of our spread where the pines are tallest and the view upstream is best? The eagle whose frequent flyway includes our stretch of the river? The yellow-orange dance of flames in our fireplace theatre, with the luxuriant expanse of wildness out there beyond our windows?—Can we actually leave all this, and so much more?!

Yes, a tough but wise decision. We're "coming inside the stockade," we remind ourselves. We'll find friendly warmth there. Protection from the disquieting "What if's" that steal into the consciousness in the dead of night. We'll be within sight of neighbors. We'll sense a comfort and assurance in human community. We'll be minutes away from our church and circle of friends, rather than half-an-hour. We'll be in choice hiking and biking territory and close to a golf course with inviting ski trails.

We know, too, that we'll still possess a bit of "The Ranch." In the future, when we swing into our city driveway, the view will sometimes segue into a winding, pine-bordered approach, and a tawny, fox-like dog will come racing down the gravel, ears laid back in her all-out sprint to greet us.

And at nighttime—especially on moonlit nights—when we glance out our windows, the line of pleasant homes across the way will often do a slow dissolve into a sweep of shadow-laced space, spreading to the riverbank. And, from deep in the woods beyond the far shore, we'll hear the faint but penetrating challenge of an owl, calling from the wilderness, "outside the stockade."

VOICES FROM

CULTIVATED FIELDS

"SONGS MY MOTHER TAUGHT ME..."

"Songs my mother taught me, in the days long vanished." I often sing those lines to myself, and with feeling—although actually, my mother never taught me any songs.

Not once do I remember my mother singing around our home, or humming, or expressing herself musically in any way. She wasn't one to share her inner thoughts very much, so I don't know how much pleasure she found in music, or in all the "joyful noise" the rest of us made throughout the household.

The chief maker of "joyful noise" in our family was my father. Every morning he poured out song, from the moment he climbed out of bed until he sat down to his "first cup of coffee that puts sparkle in my eye."

Through all the dark years of the Great Depression, when Dad's small business threatened to go under, he'd greet the dawn with a hearty and defiant medley. More and more I marvel at that, as the years drift by. And I wonder, now, if I adequately expressed my admiration and gratitude before it was too late.

My businessman-singer-poet sire never had voice training, but he carried a tune well and he performed with panache. He sang old ballads he'd learned as a boy, fragments of operatic arias, and purple passages by Victor Herbert, Franz Lehar, and Sigmund Romberg. He also sang ditties of his own composition.

Remember the torch singers who agonized over shattered romance in the early 1930s? Libby Holman and Helen Morgan are two I recall. Dad was turned off, yet amused, by their melancholy ululations and would sometimes burst out with a long, single-note wail of anguish, then grin at us and say with faked pride, "That's *my* torch note."

A Victrola with handsome wood grain dominated the

northwest corner of our front hall. In its cabinet was a row of Victor Red Seal records. What a musical feast: Enrico Caruso, Madame Schumann-Heink, Lotte Lehmann, and others. One record held special fascination for me, "Indian Lament," by Anton Dvorak. That piece drummed out a haunting sadness, and sometimes I would circle in somber shuffle to the mournful throb of music. "Indian Lament" hasn't fallen upon my ear in over half a century, but its eloquent pathos still beats clearly in my mind.

I often take the memory trail back to the kitchen table on the sunrise side of my childhood home and join the circle of parents and children. The fragrance of coffee and bacon, mingled with lively chatter about music, permeates the atmosphere. "'Claire de Lune' is too wispy, too vague," says Dad, to provoke argument. "But that's exactly what moonlight is!" comes the rebuttal. "Wagner is too dramatic, too much thunder," someone opines. "Ah, but what majestic thunder!" Dad rejoins. "As for Debussy..."

"Smaller bites! Chew thoroughly!" Mother breaks in. She had a watchful eye, and strong opinions about nonmusical things.

Nonmusical though she might have been, my mother made joyful noise in her own way, more subtle and indirect. She created an inaudible harmony, a flow of tranquility within our home—except in rare times when Dad's joshing or debate would arouse her Danish dander and strike blue-green fire in her eyes. In even rarer times, he'd flare back at her, and we'd have a brief but intense episode of Wagnerian thunder. But such storms were seldom and short-lived.

There was a kind of lyrical quality in the neat household my mother kept. And when she was pouring her artistry into preparing a meal, a "concord of sweet sounds" drifted from her kitchen: a soprano chime of glass against glass, a spirited beat of tablespoon against mixing bowl, a percussion of pot and pan and skillet, high and fluid notes of steaming teakettle, the contralto whir of food mixer, all honing a razor edge on our appetites.

And what a symphony of flavors we found in the dishes she served: bright yellow Danish dumplings; flaky Danish pastries, replete with cinnamon, nuts and dates; tempting mounds of "Eggs ala Goldenrod"; pies with melt-in-your-mouth crusts, dusted with powdered sugar.

In such ways, our mother created her own kind of music—soothing though silent tones expressing rich nourishment, spic-and-spanness, and comfort, intermingled with fragrance and security. Rhythms of care and understanding echoed ever so softly through her home, bringing us reassurance and contentment. She harmoniously set our world in motion for us, each morning—and those gentle rhythms are a part of our pulse beat today.

No, we never heard mother sing, but she created a certain music that still drifts across the years to reach us. Keats said it all: "Heard melodies are sweet, but those unheard are sweeter."

To this day I tend to orient myself by using my mother's kitchen as the pole star. East is where her breadboard and flour bin were. West is where her pantry was, beside her stove that poured forth a thousand different fragrances. South is where her table stood—the site for all our breakfasts, with morning sunlight streaming in upon us.

Songs my father taught me were rollicking, exulting, stirring. Songs my mother taught me elude definition. But they were there! And their subtle, harmonious sounds flow through my mind today, bright as that aura within her kitchen, on the sunrise side of home—silent yet haunting songs, drifting back from the long ago and far away.

WORDS ABOUT WORDS

Words, symbols, tiny capsules of meaning—they have been one of my main interests, and my main tools throughout my working life.

One of the most significant things I've learned through years of working with language is that, as semanticist S. I. Hayakawa observed: *"Meanings are not in words; meanings are in the minds of people who hear words."* Yes, meanings can vary widely from person to person, depending upon their home environment, their education, their experiences.

The bits of meaning tucked into word capsules—into those symbols we utter, and scrawl, and string together—are *not* static. Words are live organisms! They expand, contract, take on new and subtle shades of meaning, and they sometimes wither and fade away in the environment of usage and neglect.

Many are inclined to think that the dictionary is the "last word" on words. So we run to the dictionary for precise definition. And yet, the dictionary composers are running to the general public to update themselves on our ever-changing language! Hayakawa said: "Years ago, if you looked under a hood, you found a monk; today, you find an engine." To this statement could be added another meaning-shift that came along some years ago: "If you look under a black jacket, you find a hood."

We are wise to remain aware of changing words, newborn words, dying words. No matter what our role, profession, or stage of life, we are *involved* in the important matter of clear communication. We *must* be involved as functioning members of a family, of an organization, of human society!

It is far too easy to overlook both the assets and liabilities of language. Words can help us move mountains; they can also get us buried in an avalanche of trouble. How we use the mother tongue can promote understanding or misunderstanding, cooperation or conflict, trust or distrust.

Careless communication can prove funny, as in the case of this message, circulated years ago by a corporation:

> "Executives without private secretaries are urged to take advantage of the women in the typists' pool."

Unintentional double-entendres can mean double-trouble. I still wince when thinking of the time I boarded an elevator at the lower level, and a solitary female entered for the upward ride. Since it was nearly noon, and thinking that the attractive lady might be bound for the cafeteria on the top floor, I cordially (and with pure innocence) inquired: "Would you like to go all the way?"

There are some words which, with insensitive usage, can inflame and polarize. Such powerful volatility is compressed within some word capsules that they should carry a warning label: "Misuse of this product can be dangerous for your health!" But mindful and skillful use of verbal output will help thread us through the perils, perplexities and prejudices of our working and private lives.

Then there's the sadly overused "F-word," and other grungy expletives, liberally sprinkled through dialogue on today's screen and pages. Some writers, I guess, consider it bold and unflinchingly honest to fire away with rude-and-crude Anglo-Saxonisms. They seem unaware that shock is the only value in such words—and with mindless and unimaginative overuse, shock words swiftly become as boring and meaningless as the "you know" that so many spatter through their spoken sentences.

Often, when a barrage of offensive language is fired my way from page or screen, I think about the creative, versatile, amusing, powerful, purposeful profanity used so masterfully by Shakespeare. What a contrast to today's dismal, pointless, monotonous, sheeplike spewing of vulgarities and obscenities that so often offend the ear!

Some years ago, I remember hearing a public radio interview with a best-selling author who was well into the vogue of the coarse, crude and limited vocabulary. This writer was successfully keeping up with (no—surpassing) the foul-mouthed Joneses. The interviewer asked if there wasn't some merit in helping to preserve taste and high standards. The writer scornfully said: "Everyone knows all the four-letter words; they just don't use 'em because of common agreement." "Ah, exactly," said the interviewer, "and that common agreement is called *civilization*!"

Working with words through the years has convinced me that well-used language is the mortar that holds people together—that holds human society together! Nothing is more effective than well-chosen words for boosting efficiency, productivity and profitability...and for boosting the human spirit!

And one of the best guidelines I know, for reaping the benefits and avoiding the pitfalls of language, is that pithy point made by Hayakawa:

"Meanings are not in words; meanings are in the minds of people who hear words."

STALKING A SUBJECT

This hunter-gatherer of words enters the lush and limitless word forest with senses at full alert to stalk a subject.

But today, no prey is flushed. The clean page, usually a reservoir for catching and holding rushing thought streams, now mocks me: "I dare you to rap out anything worthwhile." Even the untapped keyboard chimes in: "Don't just sit there. Write something!"

My gaze searches upward from the hostile keyboard and the taunting white void of paper. Onto my screen of consciousness comes a cluster of pictures on the nearby wall. Anything here to spark a topic?

I zoom in on a stylized painting of Montana's Big Blackfoot River, winding around a yellow-orange rock palisade to disappear in a conifer forest. Here's plenty to start a flow of thoughts. But my gaze moves on.

Directly above is a painting of western Ontario's Lake Saganaga. A high-humped bull moose looms in the shadowy bay, peering into open water where a canoe is barely discernible in the misty distance. Here, too, is thought-sparking stuff. But my eye searches on.

At bottom-right is a faded photo of my father in lithe prime of life. He stands alongside a promising snag at his favorite Iowa fishing hole—the place where his ashes are scattered today. How well I remember that battered but jaunty hat and the leather-corduroy jacket. Through non-fishing times that jacket always hung behind our cellarway door, and even now I catch a whiff of its leathery aroma. How relentless the flow of years since that dark-eyed fisherman/father vanished into the unknown—somewhere out there where the Hubble lens recently took us back 10 billion years, to the discovery of 40 billion more galaxies! Here's a likely subject. But my eye travels on.

Close by my father's image are two venerable photos of this writer, wearing the royal purple of Iowa's Cornell College. In both scenes he's clearing the crossbar—in one as a high jumper, in the other as a pole vaulter. Here at last, upon these high-flying images of half-a-century ago, I stay focused.

While the fires of competition are now well banked within me, I think back to that youthful, soaring desire to attain Olympian heights. Staring at that kid with the burning zeal, the full head of hair, the 28-inch waist, and the flabless fitness, I feel a twinge of envy. I am revisited with a sense of that old fervor and butterfly-flutters in the stomach, mingled with pungent smells of sweat, adhesive tape, wintergreen liniment, steamy locker rooms, and fresh sawdust.

Then, back with a rush comes the memory of my grim struggle with the "Twelve-Foot Jinx." I had never managed to clear 12 feet in competition. That intimidating height would inevitably drain away all my confidence, strength, and springiness.

Then, in the spring of 1940 came the Beloit Relays—the prime track meet of our athletic conference. It was a night event, enhanced by ceremony, band music, and the razzle-dazzle of fireworks.

I was caught up in the drama, and in a soaring mood. But when the crossbar was hoisted to 12 feet, I trudged up the cinder path to my pace mark with springless step and defeatist gloom fogging my mind. I sprinted negatively down the runway, but at the critical moment when I jabbed the pole into the slot for my takeoff, the whole world exploded with the "B-O-O-M!" of a cannon cracker. A fright-generated surge of adrenalin propelled me with booster-rocket power up and over the bar. "Wow," a teammate later said, "you cleared it by a foot!"

So I licked the "Twelve-Foot Jinx"...momentarily. When

I tackled the next height, without benefit of any fireworks shockwave, I had to struggle mightily to at least knock off the crossbar. No respectable pole vaulter wants to be seen soaring upwards and under the bar!

I recall, too, later in the spring of 1940, losing some of my zeal and suffering lacerated flesh and psyche when a bamboo vaulting pole broke under me in mid-ascent.

Today, the flesh pad of my left (takeoff) foot is paper-thin, due to 12 years of pounding the cinders. Yet, even though I require orthotics, I find deep pleasure in recapturing a bit of that razor-sharp desire, the team camaraderie, the rousing (sometimes bawdy) sing-alongs on the return bus trip, the glowing triumph of bringing home a gold medal for "fair old Cornell," and for my steady girl on campus.

A hunter-gatherer of words, when stalking a subject, can find likely quarry in any direction he looks, or reflects. The possibilities are endless: within the room, beyond the window, deep in the corners of the mind, or in a cluster of pictures on the wall.

"THE MELODY LINGERS ON"

It was a powerful and bewildering moment in my childhood. And far later I came to realize that it signified something to be grateful for.

In the early '30s, my sister and I went to the theatre to see the film, "One Night of Love." And in the unforgettable sequence when Grace Moore sang the "One Fine Day" aria from "Madame Butterfly," strong feelings welled up inside me and started a flow of tears.

I was startled and ashamed. Boys weren't supposed to cry—especially over music! I was the fastest runner and best punter in our neighborhood, and it was my soaring ambition to become an Olympic pole vaulter. It didn't seem right that Grace Moore and Giacomo Puccini had made me cry.

My love for music is strong, deep...and uneducated. When I struggle through an unfamiliar hymn in church, the notes clearly explain that my voice should go up or down—but I can only guess as to precisely *how* far up or down. My ardent but untrained ear undoubtedly misses many a musical technique and nuance, but then nobody is more deeply moved or more highly transported by music than I am. Not even John Williams or Zubin Mehta!

When particular sounds of music drift into my consciousness, life undergoes wondrous changes. Memories rush in, and again I am seated with my family at our kitchen table, with lively talk about music flowing around our circle.

Much of our talk and debate was stimulated by "The Northwestern 400 Hour," broadcast then each morning throughout the midwest from WMAQ, Chicago. It was enriching fare. The "400 Hour" host (there were no "disc jockeys" in those days) was Norman Ross—"Uncle Normie" as he called himself—a former Olympic swimmer and impassioned classical music buff. The program's opening theme was Tchaikovsky's "Sleeping Beauty Waltz," which turned on 300 watts of sunlight for us, even on the greyest of mornings.

Uncle Normie chatted about classical music in an unclassical, down-home way, with enthusiasm resounding through his crisp baritone. His selections covered the whole range of human emotion: from exultation to sadness...from reverence to lusty celebration...from brassy bombast to muted serenity. Everything from requiems to rhapsodies. Overtures that brought our pulses up to near-aerobic beat. Waltzes that put wings on our spirits. Majestic themes that "you could whistle on the way home."

There was nothing highfalutin about Uncle Normie. He never looked down his nose at pop music. He hadn't a shred of uppityness in him; only free-wheeling, contagious enthusiasm. "Here's a number that'll have you jumpin' in the aisle," he said when introducing Ravel's "Bolero." And as the music began to rise from its almost sedate beginning, its intensity slowly mounting with the rhythm of its over-and-over-again theme and incessant drumbeat, the magnetism growing ever more powerful in the thrilling ascension, my father and sister and I were compelled to leave the table and hover at the radio, swept up in the tumultuous climax.

What a way to start each day—with Ravel, Chopin, Debussy, Wagner, Verdi, Mascagni—especially in that gloomy time of the "Great Depression." Fear darkened our horizons then, with my father's small business threatening to dissolve. But reliable as dawn, the "400 Hour" brightened our skyline each morning. What fears could be dark enough to subdue the brightness of "The Poet and Peasant Overture," or the intermezzo from "Cavalleria Rusticana"!

That morning radio hour and Uncle Normie's style as host did much to sharpen and expand my sensitivity to fine music. Nothing equals an early and liberal exposure to classical music, reinforced by the power of contagion rather than compulsion. That frequent announcement, "Here's a number that'll have you jumpin' in the aisle!" had a way of grabbing the attention!

That family circle of mine has long scattered on the wind. My father and mother are gone. Grace Moore is gone. Uncle Normie is gone. Those Northwestern 400 trains that once streaked along the rails are gone. But, oh, how those "400 Hour" melodies linger on: "Sleeping Beauty"..."Siegfried's Rhine Journey"...The "Pathetique" Symphony...and many more.

Of course, I fell woefully short of becoming an Olympic pole vaulter. But then I am continually lifted to Olympian heights on the soaring power of music. I am continually swept back to that harmonious circle in my childhood home—back to fresh and joyous sensations.

The melodies will *always* linger on, drifting in from long ago and far away, faintly heard, yet poignantly clear—like a Wagnerian descant with its haunting, mystical voices.

STAY TUNED TO THE BOOK NETWORK

My 82-year-old sister's voice trembled with fervor over long distance—"I've just finished a new Charles Dickens biography. You've *got* to read it!" What a role model, my sis. When I'm into my eighties—even nineties!—I hope and expect to be able to enthuse as intensely over a good book.

Thanks to our father, my two sisters, a brother, and I grew up in a home resounding with recitations from Dickens, Shakespeare, Keats, Byron—you name 'em! Dad, whose formal education in Pittsburgh was terminated by rheumatic fever at the 6th grade, was a natural-born scholar with an ear finely tuned to the music of words.

Somehow, Dad managed to lure me away from boyhood excursions with Zane Grey, James Oliver Curwood and Edgar Rice Burroughs, and steer me into deeper seas. *"Great Expectations"* was my first Dickensian voyage, with Dad as navigator, and he tried to bestow upon me the nickname of that story's main character, "Pip" (for Phillip). But Mother put her foot down: "No son of mine is going to be called *that!* 'Pip' is a disease chickens get!"

Today, with an average seven hours daily of TV viewing in American homes, how many give a thought to the power of the printed word? Books inform, inspire, and spellbind. They transport us to unknown realms. They launch us into intimate conversation with brilliant minds of past and present.

Sure, there's good stuff on TV—maybe five or ten percent of its output. But there's nothing like the printed word to set the imagination afire, and, oh, what a glow! A fine book needs no camera razzle-dazzle. Its humor needs no laugh-track. Its drama needs no thunderous chords. *And*, a book is happily devoid of commercials with their soothing, sexy, synthetically personal voices, urging us to buy what we don't need!

When reading, I'm as fascinated in how something is said as in what is said. I guess I'm more a style buff than a plot and action buff. My respect for style convinces me that finely crafted words are not to be tinkered with. Certainly, much written material benefits from condensation, but in my mind, a condensed version of fine literature is akin to a skeletal x-ray view of Sophia Loren.

When I read a remarkable passage, it always arouses wonder: "How did that perfect choice and arrangement of words ever come about?!" E. B. White, in his classic *"Elements of Style,"* similarly wonders:

> *"What ignites a certain combination of words, causing them to explode in the mind?"*

Each time I ponder a shining phrase (*"...he marches to the sound of a different drummer"* or *"...sleep that knits up the raveled sleeve of care"*), I marvel that before such expression exploded within the writer's mind, *it didn't exist!* How did Abraham Lincoln come to avoid the humdrum "Eighty-seven years ago" in favor of *"Four score and seven years ago..."*?

Unlike those compelled to climb a mountain "because it's *there*," a writer is compelled to ascend to peak expression because it *isn't* there.

Dawn is my favorite time for savoring fine writing, when the world and the mind are fresh...and so is the coffee. In the stillness of succeeding sunrises, I read the late Wallace Stegner's *"Where the Bluebird Sings to the Lemonade Springs,"* a book on living and writing in the West. The Great West always loomed like the High Sierra on Stegner's mental horizons. And he said it so well: *"The smell of distance excites me, the largeness and the clarity take the scales from my eyes."* Books such as this one, or Norman MacLean's *"A River Runs Through It,"* deserve a special, meditative time for absorption.

On a February jaunt, my wife and I packed along some library books-on-tape, and what spice they add to traveling! But when you're threading a city's freeways, it's smart to concentrate more on the turn of the road than on the turn of the plot. *"Moby Dick"* plunged me into one whale of an error when I missed our ramp at Knoxville!

In this jet-speed age, it's still wise to switch to the slow lane when settling down with a good book. I recall a comedian's remark: "I took a course in Speed Reading, and then I read *'War and Peace.'* It was about Russia."

Years ago I saw a sign in a Minneapolis restaurant: *"Only Slow Food Served Here."* Like gourmet food, gourmet literature is not for gulping; it is to be lingered over, as one lingers over a fine wine, slowly sipping and savoring each heady phrase.

So—stay tuned to the book network. For, as the German writer, Stefan Zweig, so aptly expressed it: A fine book is *"...a fiery chariot that leads us upward from narrowness to eternity."*

WEAVINGS FROM EMPTY LOOMS

When my wife and I signed on for a theatre and art tour of New York City, I thought about all the violence in The Big Apple, and considered taking a crash course in karate before venturing there. But we had a fine tour and came away unscathed, unpickpocketed, and even unpanhandled.

However, we did NOT come away unbewildered by some of the modern "art" we saw. The Museum of Modern Art was featuring "The High and the Low"—exhibits on two different levels of their edifice. Overall, it was a memorable revelation of art trends through the decades. But when we emerged from some sections of the "High," after groping through random spillages of color, wild and arthritic forms, three-dimensionals, and electronic dazzlers, I said: "If that was the 'High,' I'm not sure I'm up to the 'Low'."

Staring at one display, a urinal (well stained) on a pedestal, I pondered over the artist's statement, if any. Was it a special message for urologists? An affirmation or refutation of "When ya gotta go, ya gotta go!"? Was the work possibly commissioned by the Kohler Company, or a bowl cleaner outfit?

Another exhibit, a rusty coffee can holding four fatigued paint brushes, was also a puzzler. Did the artist foresee a corporate merger of Maxwell House and Sherwin-Williams?

And while I'm a long-time biking enthusiast, the sight of a battered bike wheel atop a wooden spindle failed to light me up inside.

My lowest experience at the "High" occurred when we approached a brilliantly lit glass cabinet. "Ummmm, something special," I thought. "Crown jewels?" But within that radiant setting was nothing but a row of four virginal Shop-Vacs. THAT sucked away my last shred of interest!

I came away, though, with one bit of enrichment. In the

well-known Andy Warhol Campbell Collection, I spotted two soup flavors yet foreign to my taste buds. I plan to give 'em a try.

I guess I'm still locked into the old-fashioned notion that I should be able to tell whether a work of art is hanging right-side-up or upside-down. I like the sky up and the grass down. And I like the eyes separated by a nose. In much modern art, I see only a distorted, meaningless world that I have no desire to explore. Works of many old masters arouse within me a soaring "Ahhh!" Works of some modern artists arouse an exploding "Ughhh!"

Where's the talent, the artistic vision, in plopping a urinal on a pedestal? In hanging a bike wheel on a spire? In squiggling some red lines across a swatch of black? In spattering paint around? (I remember that *TIME* Magazine called artist/splatterer Jackson Pollock, "Jack the Dripper.")

It's an artist's instinct to seek new territory, a new medium, new forms of expression—and this sometimes leads to striking accomplishment. But I suspect that with some, the prime motive is to be the weirdest of the weird, the shockingest of the shocking, the murkiest of the murky. And I wonder if some aren't hiding a poverty of talent behind a veil of unskilled, uninspired dawdling.

Some avant-garde art can send a dangerously misleading message. Years ago, when we were touring the president's home at our alma mater, he led us into a room where, on the far wall, was a huge black panel with red scrawls in a lower corner. I was about to blurt out: "Great blackboard for the kids!" when the president said: "And here's the favorite of all our paintings."

When a major art show was being readied at the University of Wisconsin some years back, an imposing three-dimensional arrived and was set up in a prominent place. After many avant-gardish types had "oohed" and "aahed" over this "statement," it was discovered to be a stack of strapped-together folding chairs intended for the Student Union. The line between art and non-art is becoming fuzzier and fuzzier!

Two of us fellow Philistines in the New York tour group got to snickering at some of the displays. Most people, it seems, repress any negative reaction to works of art, perhaps because they're afraid it would signal lack of understanding or perceptive appreciation. But why NOT express our scorn, disgust, rejection!? If enough did, we might eventually have a clearer line between art and dabbling—between those driven by artistic fervor and those whose main talent is in hiding their lack of talent behind scrawls and swirls of the bizarre.

The art world—the entire world—sorely needs the bold honesty of the child in Hans Christian Andersen's tale who, upon seeing his naked and gullible king on parade, blurted out what everyone else knew but feared to utter: "But the emperor has NOTHING on at all!"

When all our senses, sixth included, tell us that a work of "art" is merely nonexistent cloth, woven in empty looms, why not candidly declare, "But there's NOTHING there at all!"

GOOD BYE, MITCH—YOU LEFT US
"DREAMING OF A SONG"
(Written upon learning of the death, in 1993, of Mitchell Parish, lyricist for "Star Dust" and many more "Golden Oldies" of the '30s-'40s)

When I learned of your passing, Mitch, I felt a wave of nostalgia akin to the feeling you expressed in your "Star Dust" intro...

> *"And now the purple dusk of twilight-time*
> *Steals across the meadows of my heart..."*

Those phrases of yours, and many others, will linger in my mind, and in the minds of countless others. *"Star Dust"* was the song of *my* generation, Mitch, and how it "haunts our reverie"! It brings the joyous days of our youth streaming back. The enchanting blend of your lyrics and Hoagy Carmichael's melody transformed a stark gymnasium dance floor into a star-dusted glade where "the nightingale sings its fairy tale, of paradise where roses bloom."

Whenever a satin-smooth sax drifted into that wistful "Star Dust" tempo, the mood changed from jivy Benny Goodman exuberance to tender, Wayne King dreaminess. The laughter and chatter died away and we glided gently along with winged feet just a little above the hardwood floor. Somehow, you and Hoagy blended talents to lead us up the pathway into the land of high romance.

What a flow of feeling that little ballad of yours undammed—a mix of exuberance and solemnity and yearning, back when a boundless, unknown future lay ahead, awaiting our exploration.

You once said, Mitch, that writing a song lyric was a matter of "...fitting it into all the little crannies of a melody."

And how magically you filled the crannies of *"Star Dust,"* *"Deep Purple,"* *"Hands Across the Table,"* *"The Lamp is Low,"* *"Moonlight Serenade,"* and many another hit tune. You deftly tucked in the starlight and shadows of summer nights—the exhilaration that comes "when love is new, and each kiss an inspiration"—and, too, the desolation that sweeps in like a cold and penetrating fog when romance breaks up on the shoals.

"A little heavy on the schmaltz," is what many of our younger generation would probably say about your lyrics. But we romantics believe that stripping away the sentiment would be like stripping away the flowers from the garden; like stripping away the spicy seasonings from the diet; like stripping away the poetry and leaving only the prosaic, ho-hum stuff.

Could be that your sentimental words led us into illusionary realms. But then some illusions can bring vibrancy and strokes of color to our lives. How blah things would be with no sparkle, no tingle, no trace of luminous star dust!

But then, too, Mitch, you wove a sober strand of realism into your lyrics—a reminder that romance is a splendid but fragile thing; that careless neglect can wither away the magic, leaving an endless string of "lonely nights." Perhaps some of your phrases in those melodic crannies helped us to cope with disenchantment and discarded dreams; helped us to find some "consolation in the star dust of a song."

Now you have taken that final exit off the thoroughfare, to "wander down the lane and far away, leaving us a song that will not die." We bid you fond farewell as you fade into "the purple dusk," and we thank you for sprinkling a silvery strand of star dust through our world.

BEWARE OF "JARGONITIS"

Laryngitis is bad, but "Jargonitis" is worse. It afflicts far more than the vocal cords; it assaults the ear, the mind, the psyche of everyone within hearing range. Aspirin won't help. Even chicken soup won't help.

Government is a top offender, with jargon constantly geysering out of its bureaucracies. Educators also have quite a track record—and who can ever forgive them for changing plain and simple "library" into that monstrosity, "instructional materials resource center"?!

Social workers are engaged in humane work, but they've done inhumane things to the mother tongue. For one thing, they've driven innocent mothers and fathers into the cold, clinical task of "parenting." If that awful word had been circulating around back in the '40s, I'd have been tempted to exclude parenthood from my career path.

Sociologists have labeled the human family a "microcluster of structured role expectations." Just picture the warm scene of father, mother, children and cat clustered at their hearth, and over their mantel an embroidered wall-hanging expressing the heart-felt, four-colored wish:

Bless this Happy Microcluster
of Structured Role Expectations

Nuclear science created a new tributary of jargon that now flows steadily into our language mainstream. I was vividly reminded of this when I saw the following ad in a trade magazine:

"Wanted: Person to work on nuclear fissionable isotope molecular reactive counters and three-phase cyclotronic uranium photosynthesizers. No experience necessary."

A nuclear scientist friend of mine was going through a fat text with the one-word title, *ISOTOPES*. The book accompanied him to his barber shop on his haircut day, and he placed it on a stand before climbing into the chair. As the barber was clip-clipping along, he glanced at the book and said: "Oh yeah, I-*sot*-o-pes, I remember readin' about them Greeks when I was in school."

The burgeoning field of computerization has created an oceanic input of jargon, and much of it is *not* user-friendly!

Every field of endeavor coins its special vocabulary, because jargon is useful—even necessary—up to a point. Most specialization requires a bit of exclusive terminology, and verbal shorthand for easier communication about unique instrumentation and processes.

But for the uninitiated, jargon can be a formidable and confusing thing. And it tends to be overdone—or rather, overspoken. Jargon is also known as "Ego-Speak"—a form of ego satisfaction. Deep down inside, most of us would like to be the only ones who know what we're talking about. And that explains the infectious nature of "Jargonitis."

"Policyholder," within the insurance profession, is probably more accurate than "customer," or "client." But all those syllables lumber along like a slow, strung-out freight train. Besides, folks don't *hold* their insurance policies; they just file them away.

Then there's "Insurance Carrier." The tail-end of that term has long troubled me. We have typhoid carriers. And flu carriers. Must we also endure insurance carriers? I opt for "insurer." It's a little tough to pronounce, but in print, at least, it's far more lean and crisp. Far healthier, too!

What about those dusty, doddering clichés we hear echoing and re-echoing throughout the business world? I'd say that...

- It's high time we bottomed out on "The Bottom Line."
- We've been grossly overfed with "There's no free

lunch."

- We sorely need a viable alternative to "viable alternative"!
- Borrowing from a charming song in "My Fair Lady," we've long ago "grown accustomed to" the *interface*. Too well accustomed!
- Surely we've squeezed the last ounce of usefulness out of, "Between a rock and a hard place."
- And finally, I'll *level* with you—I long ago ceased to have the slightest yearning for "a level playing field."

By shunning any *interface* with vogue words, we'll speak more in our natural, individual style and less in homogenized gobbledegook. We'll be clearer, more concise writers and talkers. And we'll consistently succeed in finding—uh—viable alternatives to jargon.

THE GREATEST IDEA SINCE THE WHEEL

The spiral nebula projected onto the screen that day still glows in my mind—a silvery swirl of a galaxy, flung across the black expanse of the firmament. Our astronomer-teacher pointed toward the glowing heart of the star cluster, an unimaginable distance away in the unimaginable vastness of space. Pure excitement rang in his voice: "Just look at that! Look! *Something's* going on out there!" Instantly, his contagious excitement was vibrating along my spine.

What greater adventure is there than peering into the unknown, pondering new concepts, confronting new facts and ideas?! Again and again we have experienced such excitement when "Elderhosteling" around the country and abroad.

That Virginia professor in astro-physics communicated intense enthusiasm along with awe-inspiring facts and educated speculation. We sensed the same intensity in a Vermont professor who presented a week's course on the life and poetry of Robert Frost. And when he closed his eyes and poured forth poetic line after poetic line, he *was* Robert Frost!

A deeply personal story was told us by another New England professor. "I'd been a New York City newspaperman and a harried commuter," he said. "One evening, after an especially tough day, I randomly chose Thoreau's *"Walden"* from a bookstore rack in the train station on my way home. When the train started to roll, I started to read. Before I'd reached my suburb I *knew* I was going to change my entire life! I went back to school, got a degree in American Literature, and I've been teaching ever since, here in the Green Mountains."

Stimulating teachers are but one reason why Elderhostel is the greatest idea since the wheel. Many of us, I'm sure, look back at our brief odyssey through school, and regret that we traveled too narrow a track. We wish we'd looked into other fields along the way. Now we have a second chance, through Elderhostel.

The idea was born in 1975 when week-long courses for "older folk" were offered on a scattering of New England campuses. Today, Elderhostel is an international network of over 1,800 educational institutions in every one of our United States, in every Canadian province, and in more than 45 foreign countries. To take part, your only requirement is to be at least 55 years old.

You'll find the pursuit of knowledge in Elderhostel to be pleasurable and tension-free. No preparatory work. No exams. No papers to write. No homework. No grades. No note-taking unless that's what you desire.

Most professors seem delighted with Elderhostelers, finding them eager learners, brimming with good questions, and no discipline problems. You'll mingle with congenial classmates who come from a rich variety of backgrounds. And Elderhostel is a non-profit organization which keeps costs as low as it possibly can.

Elderhostels that my spouse and I remember with special fondness include a three-week sojourn in England with programs at Canterbury, Plymouth, and Sheffield; the mile-high campus of Rocky Mountain College at Leadville, Colorado; a primitive retreat in the forest along Crescent Lake on the Olympic Peninsula; another primitive conference center near Peggy's Cove, Nova Scotia; a handsome limestone complex along the Guadalupe River in the rugged hill country of Texas; and another center of learning in the Chihuahuan Desert near Carlsbad, New Mexico.

One unforgettable evening at Plymouth, England, an old Welsh librarian related in a deep and musical voice his vivid memories of the Nazi blitz. He told about the night when the Plymouth library took a direct hit. After the war, in the 1950s, he had broadcast the same story in Great Britain, and months later he received a huge box from Germany. Inside he found a choice collection of books, together with an explanatory letter:

> "I heard your BBC broadcast. I was a Luftwaffe pilot through World War II and I checked my personal log. I discovered that I was over Plymouth on the night you described, when your library was so badly damaged. These books are the only way I know to help repay the terrible loss we caused."

"That letter," the old Welshman said, "brought me the most heartwarming experience of my entire life!"

You, too, will find many a heartwarming experience in Elderhosteling. Give it a whirl. You'll be able to explore everything from spiral nebulae to Beethoven sonatas. Chances are, you'll find that the "pursuit of happiness" and the pursuit of knowledge are intertwined. And, chances are that you, too, will conclude that Elderhostel is the greatest idea since the wheel!

VOICES FROM

THE TRAFFIC STREAM

(Two-Wheeled & Four-Wheeled)

THE GUY IN THE OTHER LANE

You're at the stoplight, hubcap to hubcap with a car in the other lane, waiting for the red to flick to green.

Your next-door-neighbor-on-wheels hunches forward a little—and then something silly happens inside your brain. The traffic light becomes something like a starter's upraised gun. You seem crouched on a cinder track, digging your spikes into the starting blocks with savage, pent-up steam. Old devil Speed is beginning to needle you—beginning to take over the controls. "Beat this guy!" he commands. "Make 'im eat your exhaust!" You nudge up, hubcap to hubcap again.

Your next-door-neighbor-on-wheels inches forward a little—and up goes your blood pressure! A fender-to-fender sprint, and then you thrust half-a-hood ahead of your rival. A grin comes—not across your face, but crinkling across your mind in an ornery and primitive kind of way.

The competitive instinct. It puts a real kick in life. Starts the old adrenalin flowing. A good and powerful stimulus for the job, for the gym floor, for the playing field. But it has *no* business in the driver's seat. Threading through daily traffic shouldn't be a contest, and contesting behind the wheel is childish, dynamite stuff!

Sometimes, in the midst of a hubcap-to-hubcap sprint, you might risk a quick, sideways glance and discover that your "rival" is a close friend, your next-door-neighbor, your minister. And what a shock! You feel like a kid, flushed with shame when you're caught in an act that is awfully foolish, and awfully wrong. Instantly, the competitive spark sputters out—and you want to act like a mature, civilized and compassionate human being!

What about that guy in the other lane? Is he *really* out to beat you? Take a good look at him before you hunch down and dig into the starting blocks. That's brother-man over there. Sharer of your streets, your sun, your good, green earth. He's the doc who brought your first-born into the world. Second vice-president of your service club. Tenor of your barbershop quartet. He's the man whose son might marry your daughter some day. Walking down main street with him, kneecap to kneecap, you wouldn't even think of trying to beat him to the corner! So—why does humming horsepower lull us into stupidity? Why does old devil Speed paralyze our brains? Turn us primitive? WHY?

Turn on a smile instead of a spurt of mindless speed for the guy in the other lane. Show him friendliness instead of trying to show him up. Be quick with goodwill instead of pickup.

And, if the driver alongside of you does carry a challenging chip on his fender, don't rise to his whizzing rate of speed; don't fall to his wheezing rate of mentality! Let him zoom on by toward that strange goal of his—a goal that's as dim and unknown to him as it is to you, and to me, and to millions of other guys in other lanes.

GLIDING THROUGH THE GELDERLAND

We were ten "Gazelles" and one "Rhino" when we bike-toured Holland's Gelderland Rivers area—a great delta formed by the rivers Rijn (Rhine), Waal and Maas, embracing the oldest churches, castles and hamlets of the Netherlands.

The bicycles we'd picked up at Arnhem were new and robust—so robust that while they bore the label, "Gazelle," one of our bikers nicknamed his "Rhino" after hoisting it over a curb or two. The two-wheelers required us to back-pedal when shifting, which at first was as tough as rubbing your head while patting your stomach. But the bikes served us well, so we gave our ten "Gazelles" and one "Rhino" an A-rating.

At our headquarters hotel in Arnhem, The Haarhuis (yes, we joked about that name!), we packed our saddlebags and picked up our routing instructions at the tourist center, Provinciale Gelderse VVV. Then we wheeled off for Berg en Dal, 45 kilometers away, as the oriented biker flies. But we were disoriented as soon as we began trying to thread through Arnhem's tortuous traffic pattern. We penetrated and repenetrated a tunnel, circled and recircled a rotary, crossed and recrossed a six-laner that was as blurry with traffic as Interstate 90 on a summer weekend.

At last, with the aid of cordial natives, we were gliding into the quiet countryside, on a trail happily divorced from automotive traffic—until a moped sneaked up on us and zoomed by at close margin, reminding us that we had to share our path with these mechanized Super-Gazelles. From then on our motto was: "Keep right or get creamed!" Dutch drivers are uncannily skillful at giving you the near-graze, just a hair away from a full-blown sideswipe. American cyclers who don't observe our motto are easily identified in Holland; they're the ones with the frayed left sleeves and pantlegs.

While we kept a white-knuckled grip on our handlebars in

the traffic of such cities as Nijmegen, Geldermalsen and Zeist, most of our time was spent pedaling through bucolic expanses with few mechanized vehicles in sight. From the vantage point of a bike seat, we were able to savor the country atmosphere, sniff the flowers, the fresh-cut hay, the fresh-slung manure. We heard the chuffing of farm machinery, the music of warblers, and the gentle wind song. And we exchanged many a friendly "howdy" with people in fields and farmyards and along brick and cobblestone streets.

Bike touring got us off the beaten tourist track, bringing us sights and experiences far beyond the range of four-wheeled travel. It was a rare Dutch treat to merge with the landscape, absorbing it through all our senses, rather than hurtling through it like an insensitive foreign object.

Our tour was mainly in the "Betuwe" or lower river lands, where we encountered only gentle dips and rises. So it was usually the wind that dictated the shifting of gears, save for occasional inclines at bridge or ferry, or when ascending to a dike. It's a strange wind in Holland. No matter how the trail twisted—even doubled back—we always seemed to be pedaling into a brisk breeze. That old Welsh prayer, "...may the wind be ever at your back..." apparently failed to spread any influence eastward over the English Channel.

Since we knew before departing on our six-day bicycle tour that we'd be doing a lot of cycling on dikes, I suggested that we each wear a T-shirt with the slogan: *BIKE HIKE DIKE TYKE*—but the idea didn't fly.

Here and there, especially around Nijmegan, we encountered grim reminders of World War II, in massive concrete bunkers and pillboxes. And there were remnants of much earlier wars, such as the mossy, circular ruin of Castle Batenburg, with its surrounding moat, ravaged by a forgotten war of the 16th century. Often a church spire, a castle tower, or the immobile arms of a windmill would relay the first hint that a village awaited us in the hazy distance. Many a Dutch hamlet suggested a cluster of Howard Johnson restaurants. Roofs of orange tile brightened the skyline, sometimes spreading a bold orange swathe along a canal or riverbank.

We saw some sharp contrasts: snowy lace curtains fluttering luxuriously in the windows of a humble trailer home; an old gentleman tending his garden, smoking a Rembrandt-vintage pipe, wearing wooden shoes—and working away in a black suit-coat while using an electric hedge-trimmer; a massive canal boat chugging imperiously up the Rijn—with feminine underthings dancing along a clothesline on the top deck. "Wash on the Rhine," remarked a witty member of our group.

Our tour directions were in *un*plain English.   The first day's instructions said: "Go immediately left across bridge." Did that mean: "Cross bridge, then turn left"? Or: "Turn left and then immediately cross bridge"? The trouble was that we couldn't go immediately left without first going right, and that required pedaling the wrong way down a one-way ramp. As we huddled in confusion around our map, I saw a sign, "Wieldruk 1.3."   "Hey, we're only 1.3 kilos from a place called Wieldruk," I said. But we couldn't find it on our map.

Next day, as we debated whether "three cross roads" meant the third of three crossroads, or the first three-road junction, I again saw a sign, "Wieldruk 1.3." "Strange," I thought. "We must be pedaling in a big circle." And again we failed to spot the elusive village on our map.

The third day, stymied by the direction, "Turn left at the fat tree," we were trying to decide whether a particular oak was fat, or merely medium-stout, when *again* I saw posted close by, "Wieldruk 1.3." "Ye gods," I said, "we're pedaling around in a Dutch squirrel cage!"

"Where in the world is Wieldruk?" I asked a Dutch bar maid that evening in "De Gouden Leeuw" (Golden Lion). She had said that she could speak a "leeedle" English. "Wieldruk?" she replied. "It is—how you say? It is no place. It is—how much the trucks can weigh to go on the road." So all they'd been trying to tell us was that we couldn't ride a "Rhino" heavier than 1.3 tons!

Most of the Dutch people bike regularly—to work, to school, to shop, and to socialize. That probably explains their exceptional health and longevity. In larger cities we saw women pumping vigorously along in dignified dress and high heels, and businessmen biking with briefcases looped on their handlebars. I recall a snowy-haired great-grandmother, sliding a hefty sack of groceries into her pannier, springing onto the saddle and pedaling off spryly toward home.

My most delicate balancing act on the tour was performed, not on my "Gazelle," but at the teller's cage in a bank. When I set out to cash my first traveler's check, I found myself unexpectedly walking a fine line between decency and indecent exposure! The blond teller scarcely spoke even a "leeedle" bit of English, but she smiled and nodded when I displayed the check, so I signed it and passed it to her. "Now—passport?" she asked. "Uh—you have to see my passport?" She nodded, and a chill went through me. My passport was hopelessly buried beneath my outer pants, my Bermuda shorts, and my underpants, snugged away in my money belt, the pouch of which was riding along the small of my back. (I'd vainly positioned the pouch in back to avoid looking paunchy.)

"I sort of have a problem," I said. "Could I borrow your restroom?" She shook her head in puzzlement. At this point my biking colleague, George, seeing what I was in for, muttered "Lotsa luck," and walked out of the scene. To make things worse, a line of customers was briskly forming behind me.

Fearing that I might be arrested as a flasher, I took a deep breath, did a stripteaser's half-whirl away from the astonished teller, and unzipped my outer pants. While she and the customers watched in amazement, I fumbled for the zipper of my Bermuda shorts. I heard a feminine giggle—and suddenly I was all thumbs. Breaking into a cold sweat, I went elbow-deep into my second fly, struggling to reach the pouch along my lower dorsal curve. After some desperate bumps and grinds, to the tune of Dutch whispers and snickers, I managed to tug the pouch around to my solar plexus territory, but its stubborn zipper refused to unzip. When I finally coaxed it open, and fished out the precious document, I half-expected the teller and long lineup of customers to break into a cheer. For the remainder of the tour, my passport was more readily accessible!

Our pace was leisurely—25 to 35 miles a day—and we took plenty of time for lunch, tavern breaks, shopping and sightseeing. What a great feeling after a day's cycling to settle in a pleasant inn, have a shower and change of clothes, sip (slowly!) a glass of that famous and powerful Dutch gin, "oud genever," exchange talk with those natives who could speak a leeedle more than a "leeedle" bit of English, and then tackle a savory Dutch dinner: heaping platters of meat, two kinds of potatoes, four kinds of vegetables. With abandon, we ladled the butter on creamy things, and poured the cream on buttery things. And how delightful to discover, at tour's end, that we'd gained no weight—even pedaled off a pound of two!

When we winged homeward from Amsterdam's Schiphol Airport, a brimming bike-bag of fine memories flew with us: sensations of gliding through fragrant fields, forests, orchards, and Van Gogh landscapes with graceful treelines tapering off to the vanishing point.

Most deeply etched in my memory is the time spent in Ravenstine, a picturesque and peaceful village where our hotel, the Veerhuis, was nestled along the river Maas. Early Sunday morning as we cycled out of the village there was a distinct

Sabbath stillness in the dawn. We glided in meditative mood along a curving path with trees towering on either side, and the slanting sun rays glancing off layers of mist along the meadows. Westward, the trees stood vivid green in the foreground, ghostly grey in the middle distance, and gossamer silver on the skyline, where a half-real church spire stood in the misty distance.

As we glided along in silence, the faraway chime of a church bell came drifting to us from the ethereal skyline. And I seemed to hear an old, old reverence in the muted tone, echoing across a vast expanse of centuries.

It was a moment to remember. A moment of mystical linkage with the past, and with unknown ancestors. Now—many years and thousands of miles away—I still remember.

THE EIGHTH WONDER OF THE WORLD

Children are as common a phenomenon as flowers and showers and sunshine...but they are also the eighth wonder of the world. They are a more amazing expression of natural energy than Niagara, and their incessant whirlpools of action steal lots of your patience, much of your time, and all of your heart.

Children are too complex to capture with words. They suggest such a bewildering combination of things: toys and noise; perpetual motion and impulsive notion; freckled mugs, twisted rugs, litterbugs. They are clothing-rippers and jam-drippers; marble-droppers, furniture-hoppers and breath-stoppers; truth-fudgers and towel-smudgers. They're non-sleepers and non-wakers; irresistible forces and immovable objects.

Children are professional smashers of things: smashers of peace and quiet, of your best dishware and oldest antiques. And they are smashers of the most accepted theories in child psychology. In children, we have long had efficient atom-smashers, even back in the pre-nuclear age.

Children are what we adults are thankful we got over...and they're a shining, sparkling something that we never should have outgrown!

This smasher-specialist and world's eighth wonder is in special danger during summer. Whether you are a parent, future parent, or grandparent, you should know that fatal accidents involving children take a giant leap upward in the months of long, leafy days.

As a driver, remember that there is little supervision for summer play, so it's more likely for a youngster to dash into your path. Whenever you approach the child-life zones, keep your eyes extra busy, accelerate your alertness, and decelerate your car.

More than 40 percent of all biking fatalities occur in the quarter from June through August. Watch for too-young cyclists weaving unsteadily down the street. And watch for too-confident bikers who swerve and stunt and zip out from side streets. They should know better, but you have to do some thinking for them. Give them that extra margin of safety they neglect to give themselves.

Through all the spring-to-autumn days, this eighth wonder of the world will be jetting into your range of vision on flying legs, on flashing wheels, on wings of adventure. Through understanding, alertness and discipline, help make it a carefree and pain-free flight through those long, leafy, sun-washed days which become some of the fondest of all human memories.

THE PEDDLING OF PEDALING

Imagine yourself biking up one of Vermont's Green Mountain roads. You've been grinding and gritting your way upward for two miles, but there's a lot more ascent ahead. It's late afternoon, and you've already pedaled through forty-five miles of tough terrain that day. You're sweaty, hungry, bone-weary. Your rear-end is somewhere between numbness and agony. Your mind is saying, "C'mon—just a few more miles." Your body is saying, "No way!"

You struggle around an upsweeping curve. All you see ahead is more uphill. At that discouraging sight, your hammering heart, heaving lungs, and harrowed thigh muscles bellow the command: "Take a break!"

You dismount and fish the water bottle out of your saddlebag. You take a swig, wondering whatever happened to all the coolness in the world, all the oxygen in the air, and all the strength in your legs.

After your gasps have subsided to half-gasps, you mount up again, pointing your bike across the road to get a bit of momentum before turning uphill to defy gravity. But the rebellious two-wheeler swings downhill, and before you can regain control you've lost ten precious yards. Feeling like a blitzed quarterback, you pull yourself together for another try. And as you wheeze on up the mountain, a question keeps echoing within your brain: "Why am I punishing myself like this?"

That question has come to me at other times and places besides Vermont's mountainous terrain. It appeared during grueling hours of grinding a single-speed bike over hillier parts of Denmark's Jutland peninsula. It appeared while bucking relentless winds in Holland's Gelderland. It appeared while pedaling/sloshing through a steady downpour along the Moselle River in Germany's wine country. It appeared partway up a killer hill in France's Loire River Valley.

But an answer always arrives, though sometimes much delayed: For every uphill struggle there's an exhilarating downhill glide; for every interlude of exhaustion there's an inspiring view from a lofty lookout, or along a down-rushing mountain stream; for every cruel final stretch of a day's journey there's a comfortable country inn waiting with frost-cold beer and showers and congenial talk and laughter with companions around a savory dinner table. It was at such a banquet on one evening of our Vermont tour that I suddenly leaped to my feet, wine glass in hand. My biking buddies all stared at me, somewhat startled, then grew quiet to await my toast. "Sorry," I explained. "Just trying to work out a cramp around my tibialis anterior."

A number of us in our "Biking Viking" gang are two-wheeling it through our mid-seventies, and we expect to keep up the momentum into—why not clear through—our eighties. For cardio-respiratory fitness and weight control, bicycling ranks near the top. It's great for the legs, lungs and heart; it's even greater for building camaraderie, and for building that "it's-great-to-be-alive" spirit. As you pump rhythmically along, you have the good feeling that you're grinding away flab, that you're gaining more vigor in your legs, more oxygen in your blood, more joy in your soul...and more time in your life.

You feel a closer kinship with the natural world when you break out of that metal cocoon of a car. Instead of hurtling through the landscape, you blend into it—become an elemental part of it. The sun and wind beat directly on your face (rain, too, occasionally). The meadowlark's song drifts directly to your ear. The fragrance of wildflowers streams directly to your nostrils.

Imagine yourself stepping out before breakfast into a brisk, Green Mountain morning to ready your bike for the new day's tour. Gone is all the drag of yesterday's exhaustion. You're keenly aware of the buoyant anticipation within you—of the coffee/bacon fragrance drifting from the inn's kitchen—of the mist-streamers hovering over the mountain ridge, and probing gently down its forested shoulder. Above all, you're aware of the dawn's sacred stillness, enveloping you and the entire valley.

There are sermons in such mornings—and in the many other sensations that are interwoven with two-wheeled travel through many, varied corners of our world.

THE CHILDREN WHO BLOOM IN THE SPRING

Things really blossom out in the spring—flowers, leaves, rugs and rug-beaters, fishing tackle, screens, new romance, vacation leaflets.

And children, too—on tricycles, bicycles, unicycles, skates, pogo sticks, scooters, hands-and-knees, flying feet. You see them sprinting along the sidewalks, dangling from tree limbs, jumping rope, coaxing kites up into the blue, shagging flies, hopping hedges, chasing soccer balls. Whatever they're doing, they're giving it all they've got, dashing madly over the terrain as though Captain Hook were in hot pursuit!

But when it comes to the dangers that lurk just beyond the curb, think back to your childhood. Did you worry your young head over such unexciting stuff as reaction time and braking distance? Didn't your folks cram you ten times a day with "Look both ways before you cross"? And wasn't there many a time when you plumb forgot that warning and dashed blindly from the curb because Jesse James—or Captain Hook—was closing in on you, or because you had to nab Poison Pete before he waylaid the stagecoach with the bulging trunk of gold?

Kids will always be impulsive. There are always times when excitement forces natural-born or trained caution into the background of young minds. So—near playground areas, in residential zones, wherever children are likely to be skimming along the boulevards and bouncing along the walks, and poised like coiled springs on the curbs, decelerate and keep your right foot *yearning* for the brake pedal.

Be prepared for anything to happen in the child-life preserves. Help to nourish the beautiful and boisterous crop of vibrant, perpetual, and unpredictable motion that blooms in the spring.

THE CASE OF THE UNPARALLEL PARKER

My mind was roaming free and faraway as I waited in the car for my wife to finish a shopping jaunt. I was mentally on my favorite romp along the Rockies from Colorado to Montana when I became vaguely aware of a car stopping ahead, preparing to back into that rare phenomenon known as a *vacant* parking place. The spot ahead was open and ample.

Although deep in western daydreams, I noticed how the driver worried at his steering wheel like a Boston bull terrier—frantically, erratically. He had positioned himself too far from the adjoining car. "He'll blow it," I thought. Clawing pugnaciously at the wheel, he wound up four feet from the curb and sadly unparallel to it.

The man climbed out, surveyed the dismal results of his effort, climbed back in and awkwardly repeated his error. I thought about backing up a little, but glancing at the space ahead, I said to myself: "He's got enough room to park a truck!"

So, my mind slipped westward again. I was only half-conscious of the inept parker, fussing to and fro, trying to make the best of a bad job. I returned from Glacier Park to reality just in time to see him shut off his motor in frustration and clamber out of his car. Squeezing a bulgy briefcase against his bulgy body, he locked his car, looked my way and said with gentle reproach: "You might have backed up and given me more room, since you're partly into my space."

I reacted with angry righteousness...and a touch of guilt. "I'm *not* in your space. See for yourself. How much room do you need!?"

He walked away in silence. But a car length away he paused, looked back and said, "Well, you still might have had the courtesy to back up a little."

The pudgy parker disappeared around the corner. But his

last words lingered. He had somehow sounded, not angry, but plaintive—almost wistful. My indignation melted into shame. "He's right," I decided. "Why didn't I have the courtesy? Guess I was too far into next summer's vacation. As a parallel parker, he's a dud...and as a thoughtful person, so am I."

I'm glad that poor parker momentarily entered my life—or rather, backed into it with his bumbling maneuvers, his fat briefcase and his gentle criticism of my insensitivity. He started up "that still, small voice" deep inside of me. He reminded me about the importance of keeping high octane in the courtesy tank. He made me uncomfortably aware of how we're too wrapped up in our own set of wheels, our own concerns, our own destinations; how we're too inclined to regard others as challengers to our right-of-way; how others are *not* necessarily our rivals...unless our attitude makes them so!

If we were as concerned about the rights of others as we are about our own, there would be far more harmony along life's traffic lanes—and far less bluffing and bullying and bashing of automotive and human chassis.

I'll long remember that unparallel parker. Sure, he had enough room to park a truck, and he blew it. But I had the chance to make things a little easier for another...and I blew it, too!

TWO-WHEELED AND FOUR-WHEELED
TOUR DE FRANCE

The sight sent shivers down my spine. We were sitting up front on our tour bus, enjoying the driver's view as we topped one of the hills that ripple the Normandy landscape. Pedaling up the next rise ahead was a file of cyclists, and over the crest zooming toward us was a broad and burly truck. A tight squeeze was imminent!

Our driver, Philippe, spurned his brake and knifed on through the stingy space, seemingly leaving the bikers mere inches of clearance. Margaret and I glanced at each other, thinking: "You've gotta be out of your mind to bike these French highways!"

We *had* been out of our minds, the six previous days, pedaling 125 miles along the Loire Valley. But while French drivers might occasionally seem to graze your left knee and elbow, they take care not to draw blood. And most of our cycling was done on quiet backroads and sylvan trails.

With our fragmentary and fractured French, we seldom ventured beyond "bonjour," "s'il vous plait," "merci," and of course, "combien" (how much?) as we fumbled with francs and centimes.

As for costs in France—combien? PLENTY! While we expected steep prices for food and lodging, it was still somewhat of a shock to pay $3 for one cup of "standup" coffee ($4 for a "sitdown" cup).

After our two-wheeled jaunt, we joined travelers from ten countries on a bus tour that took us from Rouen southward to the shadow of the Pyrenees, eastward along the Riviera, then northward through the tumultuous French Alps and on to Paris.

We strolled the length of the Champs Elysees, and in the Place de le Concord I half expected to find Ronald Coleman as Sydney Carton in Dickens' *"Tale of Two Cities,"* mounting the steps to the guillotine in noble sacrifice ("I do a better thing than I have ever done. I go to a greater peace than I have ever known.").

It was a solemn moment when we stood on the worn cobblestones at Rouen where Jeanne d'Arc died, and when we stood beside Leonardo's crypt in the chapel at Amboise. We threaded the cobbled streets of medievalesque villages, passing through stone archways and gazing in awe at still-sturdy Roman walls and bastions. Surrounded by such antiquity, you gain a sobering perspective on your own brief life and time.

Nowhere did the famous French "joie de vivre" sparkle more brightly than during some of our evening banquets—especially in the venerable mansion, Domane de Seillac, in the Valle de la Loire, where we drifted deliciously through three hours and five courses, from wine to calorie-crammed dessert.

While the French are leisurely in the wining and dining, a mood transformation occurs when they climb behind a steering wheel—and it's as though they were on the course at Le Mans. We marveled breathlessly at the young cab driver who deftly zipped us through the insanity of Parisian night traffic. When Margaret complimented her on her driving skill, and then on her command of English, she said, "Well, actually, I'm from Marinette, Wisconsin."

We knew, at the tour's end, that we would long enjoy misty, Monet-like impressions of Normandy and Provence, of the Seine winding through "The City of Light," of the night view from Montmartre, of the reverent candlelight and shadows within the Cathedral Sacre-Coeur, and of citadels and chateaus—especially Le Chateau Chenonceau, with its graceful arches spanning the River Cher.

Oh yes, and the evening in a Parisian cabaret, where Margaret kept leaning my way and whispering, "Don't look!"

SOLILOQUY OF A HIGHWAY HAMLET

To pass, or not to pass; that is the question.
Whether 'tis nobler in the mind to risk
A car, oncoming, o'er yon looming hill,
Or zoom around, unscathed. To crash; to die;
To sleep; and by a sleep to say we end
The traffic jams, the scrapes, the thousand shocks
That flesh is heir to, in this frenzied,
High-horse-power'd age. To die, to sleep;
To sleep; perchance to dream; ay, there's the rub;
For in that sleep of death what dreams may come,
When we've escaped this mortal traffic coil?
Will there be all the madd'ning, nightmare things
That haunt us now? The brainless, speeding fool?
The brash right-turner from the far left lane?
And he who, from the right lane, veers to left?
The black-browed knave who crowds relentlessly
The car ahead? The simple, snail-like one
Who weaves, and gawks, and dawdles down the road,
While cursing, frothing drivers trail behind?
Will all those fabled, far-off streets of gold
Be fouled and cluttered by the likes of these?
Such nightmare dread of traffic after death,
In undiscover'd country from whose roads
No traveler returns, persuades the foot
To be more patient in acceleration,
And makes us bear the traffic snarls we have,
Rather than speed to those we know not of.
Thus, somberly, doth Hamlet brood and think...
Then passes *not*, below yon hill's blind brink!

VOICES FROM

DEEPER CURRENTS

UNFINISHED SYMPHONY

Our religion is an unfinished symphony—a fine but imperfect work—growing as we grow—reaching out as we reach out.

It was bequeathed to us by our forebears—a rough but shining body of knowledge, enriched with truth and beauty and inspiration. But within it were some primitive themes, some discords, some passages that failed to harmonize with reality.

We have done our best with the flaws that jarred our senses; with the dissonance of superstition; with the themes that no longer quite ring true.

We have revised. We have refined. We have added new chords, new consonance. And we shall work on, as long as a spark of inspiration remains, striving for a belief that is closer to perfection.

When, at last, we leave our symphony with those who follow us, we will say, "Here is the one masterpiece of our lives. We have given it our best, but you will be able to give it more, in the ever-spreading light of knowledge. Endow this work with the utmost of your mind and heart—then pass it on with the same, solemn challenge."

This is our ever-evolving religion—a universal symphony of being; a growing and changing harmony of wonder and praise and hope...of reason and reverence...of highest thought and deepest feeling.

And, unfinished though our symphony is, and ever shall be, we will know the warmth of accomplishment if we give to it all we are, and know, and strive to be.

HUNTERS IN THE NIGHT

It was an evening routine in years past. But more than that, it was an experience laced with shadows and starlight: accompanying our two dogs on a last romp before penning them up for the night.

"Okay, let's go!" On that signal, Buff and Schoen scramble for the door, prancing with eagerness while I don jacket and cap. Once outside, my companions plunge into boundless adventure, while I follow more sedately through darkness toward the riverbank.

From deep shadows under the pines, we step into the mystical light of open space under the stars. On crossing that border we pause, almost in unison. I lift my head skyward, straining to perceive something beyond the reach of human senses. The dogs thrust their heads outward, straining to read the more elemental things, on full alert for provocative sound or scent. The three of us linger momentarily while I ponder the imponderables, and my friends ponder stirrings of the night.

After an interlude of stillness, the dogs whirl and lunge into the dark unknown. I hear them racing toward the faint snapping of a· twig, or the patter of claws on last year's oak leaves. I study the black expanse into which my friends have disappeared, then shift my gaze outward to trace the gleaming curve of The Big Dipper and the sprawling W of Cassiopeia's Chair. I find rare exhilaration in wandering off among the known and unknown constellations. I am in rapt pursuit of—something, just as are the dogs, searching southward through the timber. We three are eager hunters in the night.

Departing the neighborhood of Cassiopeia, I range through the light years toward the realm of The Pleiades. En route, I think about the bold journeys my father and I took through the cosmic territories, from campsites scattered across the land and through my boyhood. I think about the long-vanished times, my long-vanished parents, the wonder and brevity of life.

Drifting in from the east comes the faint tire-hum of a truck, rolling northward along the distant highway. And I think that truckers, too, are hunters in the night, for their windshields reveal a generous spread of stars, and they are alone with their thoughts for long stretches of time.

I track along the vast arch of The Milky Way, roaming its misty borders for a spell. At last, I begin the return trip toward earth—toward the warm, yellow lamplight of home. Nearing my journey's end, I turn and whistle into the south for my companions of the chase. Soon they lope reluctantly in from the mysterious darkness to join me. As we stroll on together toward home, we bring no visible quarry. Yet, we have captured a vibrant joy in being alive.

Ah, those nightly odysseys of yesteryear. Now, there is but one hunter in the night. No longer do my two companions scamper off in pursuit of promises beckoning from the shadowy expanses. Nor do they come loping in from the chase to join me in the return to the welcoming lamplight glow.

Over the years, our dogs had worn a trail to our north fence line where they would boldly, but at respectful distance, monitor the activities of our neighbor's larger dog. Now just a few paces off that trail, Buff and Schoen lie in permanent sleep beneath a young and sheltering white pine.

Now, whenever I'm out roaming the riverbank on a "nightcap" jaunt, it's a solitary stroll...almost. But I sometimes sense a ghostly presence. From the corner of my mind's eye, I half glimpse the flash of a tawny ruff in the starlight—an uplifted muzzle sniffing the night smells—a white-tipped tail frozen horizontally in suspense.

Ghostly sounds are out there, too, barely audible to the inner ear: a gentle rustling far off in the velvet shadows—a muted plash of forepaws down the steep bank at the shore.

And, heading back from the shadowlands and interstellar spaces, I sometimes seem to hear, from deep in the dark unknown, the haunting voices of two other hunters in the night.

KEEPING A RELIGIOUS SENSITIVITY

When plunging years ago into the task of writing a layman's sermon, I discovered that it's a religious experience to explore your beliefs—to determine which among them are worth sharing. I found myself searching through a welter of ideas, and the elusive question was how to winnow and shape them into a meaningful form. In the midst of my mental floundering, I aimlessly removed my glasses and gave the lenses a polishing. "How futile," I mused, "to clear up the lenses in hope of clearing up my thoughts." But that brought me a theme around which to cluster my disassociated wonderings and convictions.

"What about a periodic polishing of the 'lenses' in all our senses?" I thought. "Keeping all the windows of our being crystal-clear—all the wires, the connections clean so that we see, hear, feel, taste, touch, sense the surging currents of life? What better way to keep a *religious sensitivity* alive and well?!"

But it's no simple thing to keep all of our perceptive lenses clear. There is no special detergent or silicone-treated tissue that will do it for us. It demands a certain attitude, a certain way of looking at life and interpreting the reality around us.

How truly alive are all of our senses? How much do we capture, and how much eludes us in the constant flow of experience? In a discussion at our family table, when our children were very young, we all attempted to recall as much detail as we could in the stained glass window behind our church's pulpit. Our children described vivid and specific images, but their elders had only a vague recollection of a nativity scene. Our youngsters visualized figures, facial expressions, and colors. One daughter even verbally sketched the infant's tiny hand, sharply contrasting with the mother's larger hand close by.

Children usually seem far more perceptive than do adults. All their lenses are wide and clear. Somewhere along the trail to adulthood, an affliction seems to overtake many of us—sneaking up, glaucoma-like, to narrow our range of discernment.—"And where there is no vision, the people perish."

Why do our senses seem to become more and more tunnel-like with aging? Shouldn't we grow even more alert to stimuli as we struggle toward maturity, gathering a bit of wisdom along the way? Shouldn't we become increasingly aware of the reality around us, with our senses growing more and more acute?

A logical deduction—yet many declare that our perceptive heights are in our childhood, as did the British poet, Francis Thompson:

> Know you what it is to be a child? It is to be something very different from the man of today. It is to have a spirit yet streaming from the waters of baptism. It is to believe in love, to believe in loveliness, to believe in belief. It is to be so little that the elves can reach to whisper in your ear. It is to turn pumpkins into coaches, and mice into horses, lowness into loftiness and nothing into everything. For each child has his fairy godmother in his own soul. It is to live in a nutshell and count yourself part of the infinite space. It is to see a world in a grain of sand, Heaven in a wildflower; to hold Infinity in the palm of your hand, and Eternity in an hour.

Many of us recall acutely perceptive moments in our childhood—mountaintop experiences beyond expression. Yet, looking back on some of these memorable moments, we may now see them as being rather ordinary. And so we wonder, "Did I perceive something then that is now beyond my sensory range? Or has my adult perspective merely peeled away the illusion?"

In my childhood, my father and I and several others had canoed and portaged into the western Ontario wilderness to camp on a remote lake. On a crystalline morning, the rest of the gang had gone out trolling for lake trout, but my mind was angling for some unknown kind of catch. I had chosen to remain in camp, alone with my meditative mood.

After a bit of Thoreauish contemplation, I launched the one remaining canoe and began exploring the shoreline. Gliding around a bend, I headed into a beckoning bay that was bordered by a towering cliff. As I neared the great upthrust of granite on that still, cloudless morning, I felt as though I were the only living creature in the world. I sensed a stir of excitement in the pit of my stomach.

Following a sudden whim, I beached at the foot of the cliff and started climbing toward the lofty ridge. It was tough going, and during much of the struggle toward the summit, I was mentally struggling with theological perplexities: What is life all about? What am I? What and where is "God"?

As I topped the jagged crag and stood erect to gaze down upon the blue sweep of lake and green sweep of forest, all perplexity faded from my mind. Inhaling the shining air, listening to the breeze sifting through the pines, and surveying all the wildness extending unbroken to the horizon, I felt intensely, inexpressibly ALIVE! The overpowering sensation that only complete solitude can bring. In that unforgettable moment, on that unforgettable granite spire, I was the sole being in the universe; lord of all that majestic world surrounding me.

I dimly sensed that this was a summit experience—a turning point. So I decided to build a monument on that palisade to mark the moment. I gathered stones and heaped up a crude cairn, then propped inside it a bleached pine branch so that it pointed, steeple-like, toward the sky. I then descended to my canoe with all the solemnity of a Moses coming down the hallowed slope of Sinai.

Looking back now on that youthful experience, I'm inclined to smile. And yet, I feel a bit of wistfulness, too. Did I possess something then that is no longer mine? Have my wings of sensation been clipped so that I can no longer soar to the heights I once reached on childhood flights?

Perhaps you have the same feeling when you re-examine vivid childhood sensations. You sense both gain and loss; progression and retrogression. You feel that you have gained some wisdom—more understanding—more control and purpose. And yet...there is that indefinable sense of loss.

Is it a loss of perception? Is it inevitable that our senses begin to fade, like aging batteries, as we age? Or is it failure to take time, or to cultivate the right attitude for full perceptiveness, once we're swept into the faster currents of adulthood? Somewhere, just beyond our youth, we shift gears and accelerate our pace. And while speed has its convenient aspects, Albert Einstein has reminded us that "No man who is in a hurry is completely civilized."

Speed can be a useful or destructive force, and it *is* destructive if it eclipses the slower tempo...the meditative tempo. Beauty and wisdom are distilled from silent stretches of tranquility and reflection. As an anonymous writer so aptly said...

> As one aware of beauty, I lean toward slow things.
> The best mountains and harbors don't gallop off or race
> their motors. And I have yet to hear a sunset zoom
> unseen across the sky.

We need time for contemplation—refreshing interludes in which to take—not tranquilizers—but tranquil stretches of meditation. The slow lane leads us into more majestic and inspiring territory.

Too often, life becomes as barren and unsatisfying as a frenzied trip. We rush toward our destination, not knowing what all the rush is for. We don't really see people along the way; merely blurred bits of humanity as we speed by. We do not linger to absorb the charm of streams and lakes and meadows. Our focus is upon the concrete ribbon that lures us onward, faster and faster. We feel no kinship with the villages we whirl through. And when we hurtle at last to our destination, we arrive no wiser, save for the knowledge that we completed the trip in so many hours, and at so many miles per gallon.

We *can* determine how we journey through life! We can choose to go perceptively or imperceptively; with the windows of our being flung wide, or slammed shut; with a sensitivity to gather richness and meaning, or with an insensate focus that gathers nothing of lasting value.

What will be there in the summing up of our lives? So many inhalations and exhalations? So many miles? So much money? So much status? So many rounds of golf? So many grand slams? So much froth and violence on page and screen?

Something deep within us declares that we were meant for far more than we have yet achieved, or even comprehended. This desire, this divine spark, this soul, this—call it what you will—may become faded and dusted over with years of neglect, of compromise, of conformity, of resignation—yet it still burns within us like a faint, flickering taper.

Even though we may fall far short of our dreams and our capacities, we will be enriched if we keep alive an awareness—an awe of the miraculous that is all around us and within us.

One long ago May morning, I strolled with my young daughters and sons and our collie, along the banks of a stream.

I was experiencing that buoying seasonal renewal, both directly and vicariously through the sight of my children scampering exuberantly through the budding woodland.

Then came a flashback to the image of a small, solitary, spellbound figure, standing tall on a Canadian crag, surveying a wild world far below that was all his. One tiny, insignificant being, scarcely visible in the vastness of the lake-strewn wilderness. Yet, some mental searching was beginning at that moment of solitude—growing conviction that *wonder* is at the heart of religion, and that wide-eyed sensitivity will forever keep us alive to the mystery, the majesty, the divinity suffused throughout our world.

The flashback dissolved, and I watched my four offspring soar up a greening slope and pause on the hilltop, their faces uplifted into the sunlight. And a wave of reverence crested within me as I thought:

In the days of our childhood we repeatedly hear a ringing affirmation for the miracle of LIFE. Through all our days we can keep this inner voice at full intensity—keep it from fading into the grey of insensitivity—keep it resounding through our consciousness—keep it reminding us with all the vibrancy of youth that... *"It's Wonderful to be ALIVE!"*

SLEEP WELL, O KINDRED SPIRIT

Whenever we stroll or ski the trail that circles our wooded spread, we pass a modest but well-defined mound that could be—probably is—a natural uprise. It might conceal a huge, moldering pine stump. Perhaps a massive granite boulder hunches there under the surface. Or an ordinary knoll might have been shaped at that spot by nature's whims.

But a former neighbor thought otherwise. "Notice its unnatural look," he said. "See how it stands out from the surrounding terrain. It's an Indian mound," he said with undiluted certainty. "There's one on my land, too. Ours is the highest bank along this stretch of the Wisconsin River. Ojibwas couldn't have found a better place for their burial mounds."

My neighbor was knowledgeable and persuasive. Yet, even though I wanted to believe his exciting announcement, more than a tad of doubt has persisted in my mind.

Why haven't I settled the matter by lugging a shovel out to the natural or unnatural knoll and digging down to solid determination? I don't know. Maybe because I'd rather continue to be tantalized by the unanswered question. Maybe because I believe that some illusions are better left unshattered. Maybe because I've come to see that small hillock as something akin to hallowed ground. I readily understand the outrage of Native Americans when ancestral burial grounds are ripped up by insensitive developers!

So I am determined to keep that little curve of earth undefiled. The sight of it gives my imagination a vigorous stir, starts a rippling of thought that carries me far into the past.

The mound lies in a tranquil, moss-cushioned stretch of our trail, strewn with shadows of old oaks and young spruce. It greets us with soft greenness in summer and gleaming whiteness in winter. Under a snow cover, the mound is much more prominent, making it easier to believe that an ancient one sleeps beneath that slight swell of earth.

My imagination has formed a wispy vision of the being who might be buried in that place. Perhaps he was a leader of the people, or at least a trail breaker—one who eagerly explored mysterious reaches of the "Ouisconsing" River; one who gazed in religious awe at sacred stands of pine and hemlock, and at the incessant, roaring rush of rapids.

Perhaps he was a restless seeker who wandered northward, clear to the river's headwaters in Lac Vieux Desert, or far enough south to stare in wonder at the stone grotesqueries of the Wisconsin Dells, yet unblemished by garish signs and structures. Or he might have been one who seldom ventured far beyond this valley, held here by its sylvan serenity and its bounty of fish and game.

We will never know whether or not an early woodlands dweller lies beneath that gentle rise. But I feel a kinship—the tug of a common bond—whenever I pass by that special place. I feel renewed reverence for the miraculous, life-giving earth and sky. I envision what others, ages ago, might have perceived in morning mist over moving waters, in autumn's orange moonrise; in the vast expanses beyond Polaris and the Pleiades; and in the vanishing swirls of ghostly wood smoke. I walk momentarily in the moccasins of one who travelled mystical corridors of the spirit world, guided by the vivid landmarks of myth and legend.

Whenever I pass by that hallowed ground, a voice within me whispers to the one who might be there, "Sleep well, O kindred spirit."

ON "GETTING RELIGION"

Many are the parents who pack their children off to Sabbath School each week so that they "get religion". Just how do children "get religion"? Or perhaps a far better question: "Just how does religion get *them*?"

If the process of religious education were confined to a single compartment of time called "the Sabbath School Hour," and to a single collection of religious expression called "The Bible," or other Holy Book, then one might accept the notion of spooning out "religion" weekly to the impressionable young.

But "religion," according to my well-worn Webster's, has to do with attitudes, beliefs and practices that determine the quality and purposes of our lives. Can a process with such profound purposes be limited to once-a-week sessions? Is it not imperative that religion be interwoven with everyday, seven-days-a-week existence?

If religious educators and parents can succeed in sensitizing the tender young to the miracle of life, then they will "get religion", not merely on Sunday morning, but with every inhalation! They will come to associate religion, not merely with one weekly session and one church edifice, but with the wonder to be found in every moment of being and in every corner of the world.

How to accomplish this? No educational process is guaranteed to achieve the desired results, but we might come closer to the mark if children were taught to see how religious ideas are relevant to their lives. Religious education should expand continuously as we learn more and more about ourselves and our universe. It should move continuously along that endless path toward the unattainable goal of perfection, as should all educational endeavors.

Of foremost importance, I believe, is nourishing those qualities with which most children are naturally endowed:

lively imagination and a sense of wonder. Do not these qualities represent the essence of the religious spirit? By awakening and intensifying these sensitivities, we will encourage religion to speak eloquently in the silence of every dawn and in the warmth of every good human relationship.

Yet, too easily is this priceless stream of awareness dammed up or drained away by the rush of everyday life, the unending tide of materialism, the inane babble and violence of most television fare. Joseph Wood Krutch, in commenting on the Beatnik poets some years ago, saw purpose and talent in their midst, "but there are no true poets among them" he concluded, "because they lack any sense of the *glory* of life."

Here again is the essence of the religious spirit—the soaring sense of glory that springs from buoyant imagination and probing wonder. No one has expressed more vividly this ineffable sensation than did John Steinbeck in the following passage:

"Sometimes a kind of glory lights up the mind of a man. It happens to nearly everyone. You can feel it growing or preparing like a fuse burning toward dynamite. It is a feeling in the stomach, a delight of the nerves, of the forearms. The skin tastes the air, and every deep-drawn breath is sweet. Its beginning has the pleasure of a great, stretching yawn; it flashes in the brain and the whole world glows outside your eyes. A man may have lived all of his life in the gray, and the land and trees of him dark and somber. The events, even the important ones, may have trooped by faceless and pale. And then—the glory—so that a cricket song sweetens his ears, the smell of the earth rises chanting to his nose, and dappling light under a tree blesses his eyes. Then a man pours outward, a torrent of him, and yet he is not diminished. And I guess a man's importance in the world can be measured by the quality and number of his glories. It is a lonely thing but it relates us to the world. It is the mother of all creativeness, and it sets each man separate from all other men."

What more valuable aim of religious education than to spark and nourish a sense of glory that will flare like a pilot light within the consciousness! For without this mystic perception, life would remain "in the gray," devoid of inspiring color and heady peaks of experience. Wide-eyed seekers will find a sense of glory shining within the core of Christianity and of every major world religion.

And what should religious education teach about God? In spite of long and earnest mind straining and strenuous flights of imagination, there are few who arrive at firm answers. Copernicus and Galileo modified long-held concepts and beliefs, as did Newton, Darwin and Einstein. And the same is being done by today's explorers of outer space and the sub-atomic level. As we cancel out some possibilities, our slowly expanding knowledge discovers still others scattered through the macrocosm and microcosm. Is not God, or the Life Force, or the Infinite—or call it what you will—a wondrous mystery that yet remains far beyond the reach of the Hubble's lens and our finite minds?

Regardless of what our beliefs may be, shouldn't the religious education process help us face the ever-elusive mysterious with open eyes and an open, questioning mind? Shouldn't it inspire us to keep seeking for ultimate meaning beyond the infinitude of atoms and galaxies?

And, even though we may be fired with the will to attain the unattainable, we will probably never find all that we seek. Yet, we can be assured that we will be able to push further into the unknown than did our ancestors. And regardless of what we discover, or fail to discover, the search in itself will enrich our lives. It is a stimulating challenge to realize that a vast store of religious truth is yet to be discovered—and that to seek it is the most thrilling venture that ever set mind and heart afire!

To sum up these struggling ideas from a struggling parent, grandparent, and seeker, I believe that the religious education process should aim to create a belief system that is...

- Relevant to the world that we know and are coming to know.
- Broad and flexible, tolerant of and enriched by ideas of those in all times and places of the world, who have paused to ponder what and why they are.
- Growing and changing, as human knowledge grows and changes.
- Confident in the belief that humanity has the ability and responsibility to create a far more heaven-like earth.
- Vibrant with the inspiring sense of wonder and *the glory*.

With such an educational process in motion each Sunday morning, flowing daily through the family circle, cresting within every meditative moment of our lives, we would never have to ask how we "get religion". Rather, religion would *get us*—completely capturing us to permeate our mind stream and our life stream.

How enriching that would be, both for ourselves and for what we can give to life—for is it not true that our "importance in the world can be measured by the quality and number of our glories"?

THE VIEW FROM "LOOKOUT POINT"

The high bank at the northeast corner of our spot on the river boasts the tallest pines and offers the best view for absorbing the colors and stillness of sunrise.

I often stroll out to "Lookout Point" with my first steaming cup of Scandinavian Blend to witness the drama of daybreak, to probe perplexities, and to untether my mind and set it adrift in the river's mysterious undercurrents. The ceaseless flow of waters through the first blush of light brings a dawning sense of eternity.

The mere physical act of walking out to that special place is spirit-lifting. The footing is cushiony with moss and a century's buildup of pine needles. Treading that springy terrain brings a rare buoyancy, both within and underfoot.

Far upstream, the river bends westerly out of view. The sight of any liquid or earthen trail, disappearing in a tantalizing curve, flashes a line of Kipling's through my mind:

"Something hidden; go and find it!"

With or without an alluring bend, a river works its special magic. It murmurs secrets, stirs wonderings, starts a memory-flow. Softly luminous in the day's first light, a river sometimes becomes something imponderable, streaming into the forever. In human geography, a river often serves as a territorial boundary. In human meditation, a river sometimes serves as a boundary where one crosses from the finite into the infinite—from now into timelessness.

Mornings when mist-streamers trail low over the water, their mystical swirl lures me a century into the past. I then envision a ghostly river drive rounding the upstream bend—an agile crew of "shanty boys" and "whistle-water men," herding a winter's cut of "the round stuff" southward toward the inexorable spread of civilization.

Fancy sometimes sends me drifting even more deeply into yesteryear, and I imagine a phantom canoe rounding the misty bend upriver, bearing French voyageurs or a "black robe" down the "Ouisconsing." Father Rene Menard, in 1660, endured a torturous trip from Quebec to Lake Superior, then two years later canoed into northern Wisconsin from Chequamegon Bay, and mysteriously vanished.

Some speculate that the priest met his unknown fate on the Chippewa River; others believe it was on the Wisconsin, some miles north of "Lookout Point" where a monument stands on the eastern bank in his memory. Regardless of where he disappeared, the wraith of that frail but stout-hearted priest has more than once emerged from the morning mists to glide past my sentinel post.

The view from "Lookout Point" encompasses many things both within and beyond the normal range of the senses. The river's current, except in the spring runoff, is gentle—yet it starts a powerful flow of fancy that sweeps me along for surprising distances and to surprising destinations.

A dawn journey through half-light and quietude is both exhilarating and soothing. Packaged stimulation and tranquility demand a steep price, but these coveted states of mind come free with each new day, stealing up along the skyline. The slowly spreading light ignites a glowing sense of connecting with the vast universe—a feeling both humbling and uplifting.

Morning moments at "Lookout Point" are a time to reflect, to drift along meandering streams of thought, and to savor a bracing cup of Scandinavian Blend amidst the shifting pastels and sacred stillness of dawn.

VOICES FROM

THE LIGHTER SIDE

"THE LATITUDE OF ATTITUDE"

The moment I saw him striding toward the speaker's stand, wearing a Phi Beta Kappa key, a severe suit, and a severe look, I knew I was in trouble.

He was a professor of psychology, about to address our statewide conference. Our program chairman had previously mailed me his biography and speech title, along with material on the other conference speakers, and I was to "polish it all up" for printing the program. "Some of this stuff is awful long and dull," our chairman had observed. "Feel free to whittle it down and spice it up."

So I had whittled and spiced—especially after encountering the psychology prof's ponderous talk title. The only longer title I could remember running across was the following one, naming a book intended for aspiring writers:

"How To Write a Book and Become the First Successful Author on Your Block—Or, if there is Already a Successful Author on Your Block, How to Become the Second Successful Author on Your Block...and That's All Right, Too!"

While that's a lot of book title, at least it's clear, direct, and has a chuckle in it. But the title the professor had hung on his speech manuscript was brimming with out-of-control profundity. And no clarity, no chuckle. "Whew," I'd thought after wandering through it, "this might be okay for a seven-pound thesis, but it'll hog half a page on our printed program."

So I puzzled again through the title/essay, trying to cut away the fat and find some meaningful lean. Loosely translating, I decided that the professor was going to expound on the broad and powerful effect of attitude on human behavior. This translation had brought to mind the possibility of a vastly streamlined heading: *"The Latitude of Attitude."*

"Not a bad handle," I'd thought. "Just four words. And just what he's going to talk about...I think. It even rhymes!" I had to admit that my condensation was jingly, and lacking in the high-toned polysyllables of academia. But it was clear and concise. The chairman had agreed that my revision was "on target." Thus, *"The Latitude of Attitude"* headlined the professor's presentation in our crisp, beige-and-chocolate program.

I had been quite pleased with my whittled-down, spiced-up version...until the writer of the original title/essay appeared in brisk stride toward the lectern, clearly in hot pursuit of vengeance! Even though the program chairman and I were seated at the rear, we instinctively ducked lower in our seats as the speaker meticulously adjusted the microphone, then his glasses, and finally his Phi Beta Kappa key for full display. For a few suspenseful moments, he waved our beige-chocolate program aloft as though it were key evidence for a jury. He then launched into a tirade at whoever had *dared* shrink and mutilate his title.

The prof's words slashed out like Lady Macbeth's dagger, and cut me to the quick when be branded my handiwork as "a flippant, shallow, Madison-Avenue-type nonsense." His forefinger stabbed savagely at my brief headline as he thundered, "This is *not* what I am going to talk about. What I *am* going to talk about is..." And he delivered the full load of his original title—every last ounce of cloudy, chuckleless, rhymeless jargon.

"Wow," whispered my fellow conspirator, "he's pretty upset."

"Yeah," I whispered back. "What that guy needs is a little latitude in his attitude." But neither of us smiled.

Bruising experience teaches us to handle the writing of others with care and diplomacy. We learn that long-winded and obscure expression is often an attempt at ego satisfaction. We learn that by letting the hot air out of prose and hauling it down to less cloudy, more earthy levels, we might seem insensitive, insulting, even threatening, to the hot-air generator. We learn that clear and concise expression is often deliberately avoided for fear of being thought mediocre. And we must remind ourselves that we, too, are by no means immune from super-sensitivity and over-profundity.

Perhaps it would have turned out a little less bloody if, before tinkering with that title, I had diplomatically said to the professor, "Great title. A wee bit long, perhaps. Would you mind if—keeping the essence of your meaning, of course—we tried to cut it somewhat? Oh yes, and would you mind if it just happened to rhyme?"

An approach such as that just might have prevented a storm...*if* the prof happened to have at least a smidgen of latitude in his attitude.

ADVENTURES IN FILM MAKING—ONE

Joe's question seemed half real, drifting my way through the mental fog of 2 A.M. We were out on a shoot in a supermarket, having arranged with the manager to film in the ungodly hours after midnight. Our cameraman on this venture was skilled in the filmic art, but unskilled in English language usage.

Joe was not long out of Budapest, and knew just enough fractured English to startle and bewilder. "Pheel" (Phil), he said, waving a tattered script under my nose, "how we gonna shoot deese ay-zuls?"

"Huh?" I asked behind a blank stare.

"Deese ay-zuls. How you t'ink we oughta shoot deese ay-zuls?" he repeated.

I shook my head, but the two-in-the-morning mists still swirled between me and clear thought. "But, Joe—what's an ay-zul?"

"Eeets in de screept. Your screept is fulla ay-zuls!"

"It is?" I asked, wide-eyed as anyone could be at 2 A.M. "Show me one."

He unfolded his battered-and-torn script, coffee-stained and punctuated with cigarette burns, and pointed. I squinted down his forefinger and not-so-even nail to "Medium closeup of shopping cart wheels rolling down aisle." *Aisle!* Came a glimmer of light in the somber pre-dawn.

Communication got a little better on later film projects, but it was never easy. Joe had a knack of stirring plain English into strangely-seasoned Hungarian goulash. Returning from a day's filming, we were nearing a town when Joe pointed at a sign that warned: "School Zone. Drive with Care." "Pheel," he said, "all over deese country I see dat sign, 'Drive with car.' What else you drive with?"

When I tap a typewriter key for the last time, I'll still have a vision of Joe running backward while consulting his light meter, and backflipping into a sewage sludge tank. And I'll still hear the Hungarian expletives splitting the air when he surfaced. Just as indelible is another vision, this time of Joe in slow reverse, carrying a mike, trying to back silently away from a guitarist so our background music would gently, gradually fade away. This time, he backflipped over a chair and we had noises on the soundtrack like the gunfight at the OK Corral!

Another Hungarian-flavored memory is of a papermill where we were filming a brief pulping operation that was activated only once every 60 minutes. Following his bird-dog light meter, Joe painstakingly placed his klieg lights beside a huge pulp vat. "Make this shot good," warned the director as activation time neared. "We'd hafta wait a whole hour for another take." Came the countdown. "Three—two—one—camera!" But Joe, having squinted once more at his bird-dog light meter, yelled, "Eeet's no guud. No shoot. Lights no guud." And the camera failed to roll.

Heated words gushed from the director. Lighting was adjusted and reinforced. Then an endless wait for the next cycle. "We've just *gotta* get it this time!" warned the director. "Five—four—three—" Joe hunched over his camera, and between "two—one," his glasses slid off his nose and fell far, far down, plopping into the pulp at the vat's bottom. Again the camera failed to roll.

A long stretch of agonized silence was finally shattered by English and Hungarian profanities. With skill and daring, a mill foreman finally fished the glasses out of the pulp, the director mopped them off, lashed them around Joe's head with twine—and a long, tense hour later, the camera rolled.

Joe's mangling of meanings, his long, light-meter seances, and other delaying actions drove us right up the wall of many a set. Yet, he had the artist's drive for perfection—for flawless lighting, visual beauty, musical flow of action. When we would at long last see on the screen what he had tirelessly stalked and coaxed through his camera lens, we knew it was worth the agony!

I could write a book about *"My Experiences with a Hungarian Cameraman"*. Come to think about it, why not! It would "lay 'em in the ay-zuls"!

ADVENTURES IN FILM MAKING—TWO

The cannery cookroom was extremely steamy that day. Our cameraman was steaming to and fro, metering the ever-changing light intensity. Our director was shouting instructions through the confusion. Our technical advisor was giving the eagle-eye treatment to the surroundings, making certain the camera would capture only safe and standard conditions. Cookroom employees were working and watching, their self-conscious grins clearly saying, "Gee whizz—we're gonna be in the movies!"

We were preparing to film the militaristic march of a long line of massive containers, paraded by monorail into the vaporous cookroom. Just when the director was about to give the starting signal, our Hungarian cameraman did a trial pan, then yelled, "Eeets no guud. That beeg hook—she's in the way."

"I'll move it," I shouted. Depositing my script on a rare dry spot on the floor, I trotted up to the monstrous hook dangling from the monorail and intruding into our foreground. Tugging mightily, I got it moving along the rail and was just towing it out of camera range when it unaccountably derailed, swung down in a demonic arc, and hundreds of pounds of solid metal smashed onto the concrete, mere inches away from my fragile, tennis-shoed foot!

I stared in shock at the dented concrete, then at my unharmed metatarsals right next door. Later I thought about the headline that might have been:

SCRIPT WRITER SMASHES FOOT MAKING SAFETY FILM

Things happen in film making that weren't even dreamed of in planning and writing. A production in the late '60s called for a simulated school bus collision and overturn, and an aftermath crisis of many injured students. We had enlisted the aid of a moulage expert and he created a gruesome assortment of wounds so that our scenes would be splashed with realism.

To make an impressive point for emergency medical technicians, we planned a sequence of a student being transported prone on a stretcher, with a vicious sliver of glass protruding from her back. Our expert patiently worked away, trying to get a large, fake glass chunk anchored between the "victim's" shoulder blades. After painstaking trial and error, he finally succeeded in securing the jagged fragment in a firm, realistic and highly visible position.

Just then, lunch break overtook us, and the rash decision was made to leave the moulage undisturbed, and I was to shepherd the "glass-stabbed" victim to a restaurant in a nearby town where lunch was to be served to actors and crew. I was never as uptight as when I eased the girl sideways into my car. After the tensest drive of my life, the "critical emergency" and I pulled up at our destination. When I gingerly ushered the lass, with that lethal-looking chunk of "glass" embedded between her shoulder blades, through the noonday crowd of shoppers and strollers, you should have seen the double takes!

One bit of unusual and unscripted drama occurred when we were about to film a bangup collision at a rural crossroad, down in a deep valley. The director, taking a last survey, said, "Hold everything! If a car came zooming over that hill, it'd be right into our scene in no time!" Digby, a resourceful member of our crew, pulled a red bandana from his pocket, volunteered to climb to the hilltop and serve as flagman.

No sooner was our traffic stopper in position on the hill's crown than a farmer approached in a pickup, and Digby waved him to a stop. Seeing our crew and all the commotion down in the valley, the farmer asked, "Has there been an accident down there?"

"No," said Digby, "but...there's *going* to be one." The

farmer stared at him blankly—and sure enough, just seconds later, two vehicles collided spectacularly in the valley below. The amazed farmer took in the violent scene, threw Digby another blank stare, and without uttering a word he swung his truck around in a frantic half-circle and tore back to wherever he'd come from.

You're probably asking yourself the same question that Digby and I have asked: "What do you suppose the guy said to his wife when he got home?!"

OFF THE TOP OF MY HEAD

"It's alopecia," the dermatologist told me. "Oh, yeah," I said, "didn't he play for Notre Dame?"

Soon after I'd passed life's seventieth milestone, a sudden deforestation began swiftly making my dome as barren as the northeast slope of Mount St. Helens. "There's no cure, so just relax," the doc advised. So I relaxed—except when I looked in a mirror.

Sudden baldness is a bit of a shock, for others as well as for yourself. "Oh!" gasped a long-time and wide-eyed friend when she first saw me after I'd been alopeciad, "Did you do it on purpose?"

But there's a positive side. When I first crept into church as a skin-head, at least three kind ladies kissed me, standing right there in the center aisle! And, in the post-hair stage, you find yourself exploring questions that had never before occurred to you, such as: "Just where does the forehead end and the backhead begin?"

Particularly helpful was a baldy's remark on a TV interview: "I don't think in terms of losing my hair; I think of gaining more sensitive skin for my wife to caress with her loving fingers." I've been trying to get my spouse to see it that way.

I've considered toupees, but rejected them as too fakey, and too risky on windy days. I do have a new fondness for hats and caps, though. I've got to find more shelf space, as my headwear is overflowing onto the closet floor.

When discussing biking, skiing, tennis, and other retirement activities with a young couple, I quoted the fitness fan's motto: "What you use, you keep; what you don't use, you lose." "So," Carmen said, glancing at my shiny top, "I guess you didn't use your hair."

One troubling thing is my lost relationship with my barber.

Eddie and I were good friends for more than four decades, and enjoyed our biweekly conversations. I learned far more from Eddie about my employer than I ever learned at company coffee breaks! But now our paths seldom cross. "There's no reason for alopecia to come between us," I recently decided. So I paid Eddie a social call, removing my hat on entering his shop to remind him that I'm no longer a paying customer. We had a good, wide-ranging chat, and I again learned the latest about company folk and goings-on.

Another positive—I'm perpetually clean-shaven now; still shadowless at five P.M., because alopecia is as efficient with facial as with scalp hair. With eyelashes, too. Alas, now when I'm in a romantic mood, I can only bat my eyelids.

But take heart, you bald and balding folk. There's life after hair. You'll discover a keener, more clear-cut sense of getting down to bare basics. A kind-hearted friend, sensing my self-consciousness soon after alopecia had done its number on me, said, "You're still the same *you!*"

So just relax—even when looking in a mirror. And some day you'll probably get over what I still have to get over: a recurring dream that a luxuriant head of hair has magically returned.

POSTERS POST VIVID MEMORIES!

I stared in disbelief at the letter. It was short and sour.
"I'm returning your poster, as it's unacceptable to us. You
know our rule!"

The writer was the safety director for a firm that my
company insured.   And "our rule" required one-hundred
percent eye protection for that firm's employees. So extremely
zealous was the safety director that he'd *never* display a poster
in his plant unless every human it revealed—whether a punch
press operator or a pencil-pusher at a desk—was wearing
safety goggles or glasses.

That is admirable...up to a point. But the rejected poster
was one we'd developed for February use, to honor Lincoln's
birthday. It featured an excerpt from the Gettysburg Address,
and a sketch of young Abe Lincoln splitting rails—minus
goggles!—Somewhere along the line, that safety director will
probably proclaim: "Four score and seven years ago, our
company had its *last* eye injury!"

Dreaming up posters isn't as exciting as rappelling down
the Grand Teton. But over the many years I spent dreaming,
scheming and theming posters, I ran into my share of the
unexpected. Working with posters posted some permanent
memories in my mind!

We usually used the light touch in our posters—getting a
safety message across with a chuckle instead of an agonized
scream. One such poster featured a monkey in the midst of
madcap antics—and to our bewilderment, it triggered a King
Kong-sized rage in one customer. He threatened to cancel our
business if we ever sent him another monkey-type poster. We
pondered the mystery behind this attitude as we hung a
reminder on his address tab: "Send only *monkeyless* posters!"

Years ago when Rosemary Clooney first came out with her
smash hit, *"This Ole House,"* we soon followed with a serious

poster parody, *"This Ole Car"*...

> This ole car once knew its children,
> This old car once knew its wife,
> This old car once spun out mileage
> For a merry family life...
>
> But this family's trips are over,
> Picked a dang'rous spot to pass—
> Then they saw an angel peekin'
> Through the broken windshield glass.
>
> Ain't gonna need this car no longer,
> Ain't gonna need this car no more—
> Had no time to fix the brakes up,
> Had no time to fix the door,
> Had no time to fix the steerin'
> Or to drive with more restraint—
> Ain't gonna need this car no longer,
> They've been taken to meet the Saint.

On vacation the following summer, we were rolling westward across New Mexico when an Albuquerque radio announcer launched into a recital of *"This Ole Car."* My two little daughters in the back seat, instantly recognizing the lines, burst out with excitement and one gave me a vigorous hug. I momentarily lost control of the car and we were slithering along the graveled shoulder at 65 mph. After some white-knuckled moments, I eased us back onto the concrete.

I've often played the "What if..." game with that one. What if we'd wound up topsy-turvy? And what if the accident investigators had asked how it happened? And what if I'd replied, "It was caused by a traffic safety message we heard on the car radio"?

One late November we were rushing a Christmas poster through to beat the deadline. A Wisconsin paper mill had shipped a roll of enameled poster stock to the Minneapolis printer who had our order. About the time we expected delivery, the printer phoned. "Uh, hate to tell you this, but we were unloading that paper roll and—uh—it got away from us. You see, we're on a hill here, and the darned thing rolled all the way downhill...and it—uh—unravelled all the way."

I visualized all that gleaming white paper, strewn from hilltop to valley, making the neighborhood look like a sloppily decorated Christmas tree. Then I thought of our impending deadline, and all the Christmas spirit within me dissolved. But our Purchasing Department sprang to the rescue. They had another roll of poster stock rushed to Minneapolis, where it was unloaded with far more respect for the law of gravity—and our four-color Christmas poster was printed, delivered, and mailed in the Saint Nick of time.

That traumatic experience left its mark on me. From that time on, whenever I was involved with an important print job, I'd anxiously ask our purchasers, "Are these printers reliable? Do they do quality work? Do they deliver on time? *And...*is their shop located on *flat* terrain?"

THE STRUGGLE TOWARD ORGANIZATION

"Some day I'm gonna get organized," I muttered recently when cruising through the forest of files in my den in search of a bicycle maintenance manual. More recently, roaming that same wilderness to track down a Blackfeet Indian's poetic statement about life, I again vowed to "get organized." Mine is a chronic case of disorganized tendencies toward organization!

All through my working life, I kept a heap of useful—well-*potentially* useful—information, arranged in a semi-organized way, within a file drawer marked *Mader/Mealey*. Those were the names of other company people who had previously used that filing space, and after I inherited the drawer I never got around to changing the label. So, through ensuing decades, I'd regularly get requests from our field people: "Phil, I gotta give a talk on preventive maintenance. Got any information in your *Mader/Mealey* file?"

The "Gonna Get Organized" resolution surfaces, not only when ransacking my files, but when ransacking the barn to uncover the post-hole digger or the tractor's mower belt. The purpose pops into my mind frequently—and it also sometimes appears in the form of mild-to-strong suggestions from my wife!

Isn't much of life an upstream struggle from disorganization toward organization? And, once we form a bit of order out of chaos, don't the prevailing currents start it all flowing downstream again toward the maelstrom of disorder? More significantly, doesn't something deep within us yearn for—even require—a dollop of disorganization?

An overkill of orderliness can turn life bland, leaching away the spices of variation and surprise. Too rigid patterns can hem us in with stifling cut-and-driedness. Contrast a stretch of interstate, extending in unrelieved straightness to the skyline, with a mysteriously winding and alluring back road. Contrast a severely clipped, boxy juniper with one thrusting in wild abandon toward the sun. There is marvelous order in nature...and breathtaking disorder!

An overly neat home coldly announces to the visitor: "Wipe your feet. Enter with care. And don't mess anything up!" A mildly disorganized home warmly says: "Welcome! C'mon in and relax, and kick off your shoes if you'd like."

There's a happy medium somewhere. Let's call it *Casual Orderliness*—a mix of the planned and the primitive; of the neat and the relaxed; of systematic and seat-of-the-pants living.

I must admit, though, that my filing system is over-casual and under-orderly. It took some frustrating exploration to find that Blackfeet Indian statement, buried in my bulging *"Good Writing"* file. See if you don't agree that it's well worth keeping in a retrievable way...

> *Life is the flash of a firefly in the night.*
> *It is the breath of a buffalo in the wintertime.*
> *It is the little shadow which runs across*
>   *the grass and loses itself in the sunset.*

Alas, my *"Good Writing"* file houses a heap of purple passages by every writer under the sun. Someday I'm gonna find a way to make it less casual and more orderly.

I wonder...maybe a logical start would be to set up a new *Mader/Mealey* file.

SPACED OUT IN CYBERSPACE

I've taken a tentative step or two across the electronic frontier into cyberspace, then beat a bewildered retreat. So here I am, CD-ROMless and Modemless in my uncybernated world. And the 64-megabyte question is: Where am I within the state of the art? In this dazzling information age, just how primitive is the idea-searching/word processing system that I access whenever I sit down to try and compose?

At least I've progressed from a manual to an electronic typewriter. My system's hardware is a two-toned grey Smith Corona XL-1900. Sounds sort of high-tech, don't you think? It has a user-friendly "Correct" key, too. As for database, I have a fairly up-to-speed working vocabulary, reinforced by occasional power boosts from Webster, Roget and Bartlett components. And my printer? I run off photocopies at Barden's for four cents a shot.

What's more, this writer is online and wired into the —well, not exactly the Internet, but a kind of customized network that I'll try to explain.

The cyberspot where I log in, sip strong coffee to fuel my disk drive, surf the "net," process my catch of ideas, then compose, is my den on the eastern side of our home. My spouse calls it *our* den, since one file drawer and one desk drawer are hers. It's also our guest room, since it has a trundle bed.—Whatever we call it, this multi-task station is the nerve center for the hard-wired system that I've fashioned as a hunter-gatherer of words.

In addition to my trusty Smith Corona hardware, I have at my disposal an equally trusty software system—an Andersen double-casement thermopane, opening toward the riverbank and the sunrise. This *Windows Two* is my priceless access to the "Flora and Fauna Network."

The ever-changing web of wilderness out there never fails

to snare a wealth of bytes for this writer to chew on. Nutritious thought-starters emerge from the landscape, flowing my way along the network and streaming through *Windows Two*, shining with potential and ready for processing.

Until recently, the dominant idea-stimulator out there in my netscape was a lush arborvitae—a beautiful graphic on my screen. How it could ignite the creative impulse, especially when the dawn dew on its lacy foliage glistened with sunrise colors! The conifer was a rendezvous for black-capped chickadees, whirring in to the verdant shelter to crack sunflower seeds they'd snatched from the nearby feeder. Their exuberant black-and-white action was a powerful boost for getting the best words arranged in the best way, and down on paper.

But then something sinister—perhaps a computer virus—sneaked in to infect my favorite graphic. The graceful, green pyramid rapidly withered into a lifeless husk, and I sadly dug it out and tossed the once vibrant shrub on the brush pile back of the barn.

However, my cyberspot system has recuperative powers. With the vanishing of the arborvitae, a more expansive network moved onto my screen. I now have a better visual connection with an ancient red oak, and that patriarch inter-connects with a lithe hard-maple which, years ago, flung a flaming-crimson canopy over the scene of our daughter's wedding, out there on our riverbank.

At the southern fringe of my netscape is a cluster of white spruce. The sight of the towering trio sends me down the memory ramp to a long-ago spring when, armed with a planter's bar, I toiled over our acreage and tucked a hundred spruce seedlings into the earth. Today, many of those conifers are 20 to 30 feet tall, reaching eagerly toward the sky.

Surfing the net, I now bring onto my screen a fenced-in spread near the oak patriarch—the spot that used to be a pampered garden plot. That image activates my memory-supplier, and I'm suddenly back into rototilling, liming, fertilizing, planting, cultivating and harvesting. But harsh experience taught me that weeds and wildlife are indomitable. Raccoons always beat me to the ripening sweetcorn. Deer and woodchucks nibbled away just about everything green. So I long ago settled for the Piggly Wiggly produce section and the farmer's market. Now, out on that untended rectangle, only a dab of chives, an anemic scattering of asparagus, and a wan row of rhubarb put in a half-hearted appearance each spring.

I ruefully admit that my system is vulnerable to hacker mischief. Gamboling grey squirrels intrude upon my view screen, blocking or diverting my thought stream. Bluejays glide saucily through the scene with shrill, distracting cries. But the most powerful derailers of my train-of-thought are the doe and three fawns who often wander the lanes of my information highway, pausing to peer curiously toward Windows Two. When that beautiful graphic moves onto my screen, I'm lured into territory that isn't even on the day's itinerary!

That, as best I can describe it, is my idea-searching/word processing, hacker-prone system. So—do I have at least one foot into this dazzling information age? Or am I still languishing back there in the post-Gutenberg era? Should I lug my Smith Corona XL-1900 in to an up-to-speed diagnostic desk and see if the high-techies recommend an upgrade?

I'll welcome your user-friendly opinion.

VOICES FROM

RANDOM TRIBUTARIES

A SIGNIFICANT SUNRISE

How did an Iowa "Hawkeye" happen to become a Wisconsin "Badger"? Because of the lasting memory of a special sunrise.

The natural world, especially in dawn's delicate light, has always sparked some of my deepest enthusiasms. There have been sunrises that will forever illuminate my mind: one that I witnessed from an awesome point on the Grand Canyon's north rim; one that deflected off the Atlantic to ricochet into a granite cove on the Maine coast; one that I canoed smack into, following its dazzling trail across Two Medicine Lake in Montana's Glacier Park.

Then there's a sunrise that burst upon my consciousness many decades ago—a dawning that I came to discover, years later, had spilled out a flaming career path leading me into the heart of Wisconsin.

In a sizzling July of my childhood, our family was en route from the heartless humidity of the Mississippi Valley in southeastern Iowa, to a vacation spot on a lake near Rhinelander, Wisconsin. We drove through the entire night to escape the steaming heat of the Corn Belt. The first faint hint of dawn was brushing the eastern skyline when we chugged through blessed coolness into a faraway place called Wausau.

We flagged down a dairy truck and bought milk, found a small park dotted with white pines, and spread a picnic breakfast on the hood of our Dodge. We ate in the slowly intensifying light, and I inhaled the sacred stillness and bracing air, pungent with spruce and pine. Far across the Wisconsin River, Rib Mountain rose out of misty limbo into the dawn light.

In the flow of years that followed, there were other vacations in other places—and there was high school, college, marriage, and World War II. Then, when I was making plans to re-enter civilian life, I found that a certain Wisconsin sunrise was still glowing in my memory. So I wrote to Wausau's Chamber of Commerce to ask: "Any opportunities up there for a guy who likes to write?" Soon came a cordial reply from one of the city's major employers, Wausau Insurance Companies, suggesting that I come up for an interview.

And that's how I happened to enter into a thirty-eight-year career in business communications, and became a Wisconsin "Badger."

Today, we live on the west bank of the Wisconsin River, south of Wausau. Early mornings from our spot in the forest, we see a hilltop far upstream, shining in misty radiance. And I think of my first view of Rib Mountain, silhouetted in that summer dawn of long ago. Even in those childhood years, I was already shaping a dream of living someday in some wild place on lake or stream. And that dream was answered by my memory of a Wisconsin sunrise—the luckiest sunrise of my life! For it led to a job with opportunities "for a guy who likes to write"—and to where we finally found our "wild place" along a stream.

"WHAT'S IN A NAME?"

No music falls as melodiously on the ear as does the sound of our own name. Those familiar labels we go by are far more than mere sounds in the air or symbols on paper. Magically interwoven with our name is the entire fabric of our being; all our yearnings, struggles, triumphs, dreams and disappointments; all our ancestors, children and future descendants. Mysteriously wrapped up in that brief verbal package is everything we've been, and are, and hope to become.

Have you noticed how people well-versed in the social arts will often, upon first learning your name, repeat it in their very next sentence? That helps engrave your name on their mind, and it also touches off a warm feeling inside of you. You're inclined to think, "He's a pretty nice guy," even if you know he's trying to sell you something.

We've all learned—sometimes the hard way—the importance of accurately spelling and pronouncing the names of those we deal with. "To err is human"—but *superhuman* performance is demanded when it comes to the names of customers and prospects. Just a smitch of carelessness here might lead to a good-natured chuckle—but it might also lead to riled feelings, a lost sale, even canceled business.

Alas, glitches have a way of creeping in, no matter how hard we try. When I first met a writer named Faith at a communications conference, I tried the memory-reinforcement technique of relating her name to the familiar phrase, "Faith, Hope and Charity." It worked—except that whenever our trails crossed in the future, I fear I called her "Hope" more than "Faith." And more than once, I was at the brink of calling her "Charity."

Names can booby trap us in unexpected ways. Years ago, when chatting with a group at a conference, I half heard a conversation to my left about frontier lawman, Wyatt Earp.

Turning to the stranger on my immediate left, I said, "Earp—isn't that the darndest, gosh-awful name you ever heard!? By the way, my name's Carspecken." "Yeah?" he said. "Mine's Earp."

Most of us who are pinned with names a syllable or two out of the ordinary eventually become a little thick-skinned about bloopers. Uncommon monikers tend to make their owners more tolerant of a bit of slippage, it seems.

"Carspecken," you can be sure, is often bent, twisted and tortured! Letters have drifted to my "In" tray addressed to "Corspacken," Cornspuhen," and "Carstincken." At the top of the list, though—or is it the bottom?—is the memorable misfire, "Phil F. Corkspoppin." That called for uncorking a bit of champagne!

After writing a few speeches for one of my earliest company bosses, he introduced me at a conference as "the department's ghost writer." Whereupon a witty colleague dubbed me "Carspooken." To this day I'm occasionally called that...or "Spooky" for short.

Then there was the colleague who, after I began getting into film work, branded me "Cecil B. DeCarspecken."

An east coast firm once sent a letter to my company, addressed for the attention of "Phil Myberry." Since there was no "Myberry" within our company ranks, the letter drifted here and there, finally washing up on my desk, since it concerned one of our company's films. I stared long and hard at that name, wondering: "Myberry—Carspecken. How could anyone be that far off-track!?" But when I pronounced the odd name half-aloud, "Phil Myberry," it came to me in a flash: "Phil Myberry—*Film Library*!"

Old, but still somewhat painful, is the memory of a freshman week party I attended in college, where I met a Howard and a Sid, and carefully tucked their names away in my memory bank. One of the two lived in a dorm near mine, so nearly every morning en route to breakfast I'd meet him along the campus walk. "Mornin' Howie," I'd say. "Mornin' Phil," he'd reply. This cordial exchange went on through the entire school year. Then, on the very last day of spring semester, when we again met on campus, I said, "Mornin' Howie." And he answered, "Mornin' Phil. Uh, by the way, the name's *Sid*."

THE MANAGEMENT OF MORNING

We all frequently wonder how well we're managing our work, our leisure, our budget, our diet—but how about the management of our mornings? If we see Act One of the day as a humdrum thing or a frantic rush hour, then our mornings are managing us!

The first step in sound morning management is to cultivate an artist's sensitivity to the ever-changing charisma of dawn; to think of daybreak as a rare aperitif to be slowly sipped and never gulped. The drama of sunrise has inspired many a rhapsodic expression—on musician's score, writer's manuscript, and painter's canvas. "Dawn," according to some of our sensitive writers, is the most beautiful word in our language.

Of course, there's an "op-ed" page with opposing viewpoints on the day's Act One. An old Scottish ballad, for instance, declares that...

> "...when the dew is dewin'
> And it's murky overhead,
> Ah, it's nice to get up in the mornin'
> But it's nicer to lie abed!"

And here's another negative opinion on morning that I've heard:

> "All I know about the speed of light is
> that it gets here too soon in the morning."

I'm about ninety percent "morning person." Since I'm not innately inclined to leap joyously out of bed at the blare of the alarm clock, I must rely on the booster battery of willpower.

I follow a precise ritual that helps me resist the temptation "to lie abed" a little longer.   I conjure up the vision of coffee—strong, chocolate-brown, steaming from my favorite cup—as a lure to draw me out of bed and troll me along a beeline into the kitchen to grind the beans and get the brewing process going.

Next, my ritual calls for an exercise routine to give the muscles a gentle stretch, shed drowsiness and flab, and spark more cognition in the brain chamber.   Then it's into the shower, where a stint of splashing and sudsing leads to another key step—a health fad I've been hooked on since childhood. Gradually, masochistically, I change the water from hot, to warm, to lukewarm, to cool...and then to all-out cold. There's nothing like an icy deluge for getting the spirits up to full throttle!

When you step out of a cold shower into a warm, rich coffee aroma, you are ascending to the day's peak period. With breakfast tantalizing your nostrils, and dawn spreading its colors and crisp shadows outside your eastern windows, you find that all of yesterday's problems pale into insignificance. All's right with the world!

My earliest memories are focused on the magic spell of daybreak—particularly when embarking on family vacations long before sunup.   As we headed out in our Studebaker toward far horizons, I soaked in the wondrous progression of dawn, evolving out of darkness. The slowly rising action held me spellbound, from the imperceptible fading of the stars to the climactic first glimpse of the sun's luminous sliver on the skyline.

Looking back now, I seem to see all the mornings of my childhood as sunfilled—the light flooding our breakfast table to burnish the toppings of my mother's Danish pastry, and to make still more glorious her golden omelets.

There was many a sunless morning, of course, but their gloom was dispelled by my father's blithe spirit.   A one-hundred-percent "morning person," he almost invariable greeted the dawn with song and poetry and banter. His lively celebration nudged us out of slumber and into the flow of the new day. I can still hear one of his homespun verses ringing through our home...

> *When the sun shines through my window,*
> *I feel just like a lord!*
> *Haven't got much money,*
> *And there's things I can't afford—*
> *But when the sun shines through my window,*
> *I feel just like a lord!*

What a priceless gift—to be able to plunge spontaneously into each new dawn with exuberant words and music!

My mother and my father were excellent managers of their mornings. They made their children aware that daybreak comes magically packaged in rare colors and in sacred stillness blended with haunting bird chorales. They encouraged us to breathe deeply of morning's tranquility, to cherish it as a listening and a meditating time. They opened our eyes to a radiance that I still see, and revere, in each new dawning.

"FIRST, YOU GET MARRIED!"

We had biked a loop on San Juan Island off the Washington coast—no great distance, but we'd topped some Swiss-style hills. Our aches had been consoled by a hot-as-you-can-stand shower. We were deep in cushiony chairs after long hours on unyielding bike saddles. And we were toasting our 48th wedding anniversary.

"Here's looking at you, kid," I said in my best Bogart manner. Then came a rap on our door and a shout: "Hey Phil and Margaret, come take a look!"

My protesting leg muscles and I struggled to the door. I opened it into a shockwave of "Happy Anniversary!" from our thirty bike-tour companions. Our aches did a fast dissolve as we stared at the cluster of smiling faces behind upraised champagne glasses, and gaudy paper hats perched where bike helmets had been but an hour before.

That unexpected celebration out in the strait along Vancouver Island is forever in our memory bank. And so is a discussion we had in the midst of the merriment.

"Forty-eight years! What's your secret?" The question came from a vibrant Colorado pair who had been living together, unmarried, for several years. He was a personable, athletic physician. She, along with Crater Lake and the Cascades, was the most beautiful sight we'd seen on our trip. Her marriage had ended with her husband's death. His had ended in "an awfully expensive divorce," as he put it. They seemed a most harmonious couple, yet were apparently shying away from marriage.

"Our secret?" I replied. "Well, I guess we just lucked out." But my not-so-reticent spouse said, "First, you get married." "Oh no," I thought to myself, "she's going to deliver the full load!" And she did, but with a conviction that had the "significant others" listening intently.

"Making a commitment makes you determined to keep a permanent relationship," she said. "It helps you change from an 'I' to a 'We' attitude." And, with the champagne and festivity flowing around us, we continued a candid, searching discussion.

Why do so many avoid the marriage contract today? Should it contain "standard exclusions" as do insurance contracts? Are there intangibles beyond trust and loyalty that either hold a couple together through life's capricious currents, or that work insidiously to split them apart?

Kahil Gibran urged that "there be spaces in your togetherness." I recall a friend of mine saying about his wife, "I not only love Jan, but she's my best friend." Perhaps these are some of the essentials for enduring love which, "like light, grows dearer toward the dark," as Archibald MacLeish expressed it.

What causes about half of all marriages to fail? Taking each other too much for granted? Selfishness? Letting the communication line go dead through neglect? Who has the valid answers? Theologians? Ann Landers? Dr. Ruth? Rodgers and Hammerstein?

"First, you get married." Did that not-so-subtle opener have any influence on that fine Colorado pair? Perhaps, because several years later, they sent us an announcement of their marriage. Good news, because they seemed ideally matched, devoted, and brimming with joie de vivre. We hope it continues that way for them.

The jovial/serious celebration of our 48th, at Friday Harbor on San Juan Island, looms in memory as do the sea stacks thrusting skyward from the Pacific along the majestic coastline.

It was a time for rejoicing, reminiscing, soul-searching. And a time for wondering, "How lucky can we get!?"

"TO SLEEP...PERCHANCE TO DREAM"

How strange—those lands we are sometimes flown to by our dreams—enchanting, bizarre, funny, frightening places! The subconscious is an unpredictable travel agent whose services are free, but who sometimes books us on journeys that are anything but sunny and serene.

I come from a line of hyperactive dreamers. Nightmares often galloped through my father's mind, and our home would sometimes reverberate with his yells of terror.

When my father was a boy in Pittsburgh, he had an older brother living in Iowa. One dark night, Dad awoke screaming in horror from a dream revealing his brother, sprawled lifeless on blood-stained pavement. "It was just a bad dream," his parents assured him. But the next morning a telegram from Iowa announced that on the previous night, Dad's brother had taken a fatal plunge down a flight of icy steps.

Probably due to his many tormenting dreams, my father would always wish his children, and later his grandchildren, dreams about "birds and butterflies and flowers."

My older brother's conspiring subconscious usually ignored the birds, butterflies and flowers theme, in favor of hair-raising action. One summer night when he was bunking on our screened-in porch, the 2 A.M. silence was shattered by shrieks, bangs, and clatters. A malevolent dream had put my brother in the driver's seat, and he was descending steep mountain switchbacks when the steering wheel broke. On the verge of plunging over a cliff, he overturned his bed, smashed an end table, destroyed a lamp, and kicked out a screen!

My dreams seldom nudge me into such violence, but an exception was the nightmare that unleased a savage dog upon me. I aimed a kick at the lunging beast and dented our bedroom wall. For a week I limped around with a swollen, deep-purple toe.

The closest I've come to a telepathic dream such as my father's was on a night in the Colorado Rockies. My dream brought a long-time friend, Doris, waltzing into my office with an overflowing carton and saying, "Phil, I'm in a rush. Here's a list of guest names, invitations, and name tags for a party we're having soon. It's all a mess, but I know you can straighten it out." And without even an advance "thank you," she dumped it all on my work-loaded desk, exited, and left me smoldering. I was already engulfed in urgent work, now this unexpected deluge—and besides, she hadn't even invited me to her party!

Next morning at breakfast, we chuckled over the weird dream, packed the car, and headed homeward. Late that afternoon, we checked into a motel in North Platte, Nebraska. I was unloading the car when "Well, look who's here—Phil Carspecken!" sounded behind me. I turned around and there was Doris! She and her family were headed west, and in the same hour of the same day, in the same Nebraska town, were checking into the same wing of the same, multi-wing motel! Coincidence? I suppose. But I can't help wondering.

Remember the full-service days when your windshield would always be washed at gas stations? Back then I dreamed that a colleague and I were peddling a product for gas stations. So, while I'd make my sales pitch, my partner would soften up the prospect by taking bucket, sponge and squeegee, and washing the station operator's windows. "Pretty clever twist," I told my subconscious when I awoke.

My most terrifying nightmare? I suppose it was the one that put me center stage in a play that I had written. Following my script, I grabbed a pistol, supposedly loaded with blanks, and shot the villain. He crumpled to the floor, *really* dead. As the police were dragging me away, I kept screaming: "No!—No! Please—I'm innocent! This isn't the way I wrote the script!"

My subconscious never quits. I recently dreamed that a parking lot attendant demanded $22 for only an hour's parking. I was not only outraged, but short of money. So, to settle the balance, I peeled off several slices from a package of bacon and the attendant made me "endorse" each slice with my bona fide signature.

That whimsical travel agent of the subconscious sometimes flies us into idyllic environs and circumstances. But we're often dispatched to dark and dreaded places. On returning from such journeys, I think wistfully of my father's wish for tranquil dreams about "birds and butterflies and flowers."

INNER THOUGHTS ALONG THE INNER PASSAGE

"What was your standout experience?" friends asked, after my wife and I, along with my two sisters and their spouses, returned from an Alaskan cruise. My answer always startles them: "Flushing the john in our stateroom."

While the flush of an ordinary john brings a fair-to-middlin' gush and gurgle, it seems a pitifully puny sound since flushing on the *MS Nieuw Amsterdam*—like a two-piece ensemble alongside the Boston Symphony at full crescendo. The first time I pressed the button, somewhere northwest of Vancouver, there was a suspenseful silence, then an almost inaudible hum that slowly, tantalizingly intensified like Ravel's *"Bolero"* to a climactic "Kuuurrr-Whooooock!"

It left me speechless with awe. From then on, whenever I'd press the button, I'd bellow, "Fire One!"

Our ship's captain was a ramrod-straight Dutchman, lean and laconic. In the midst of an evening performance of song and dance in the Stuyvesant Lounge, his bass monotone broke in over the P.A.: "Ladies and chentlemen, I haf an announcement. We are chust now leaving the shelter of Vancouver Island and entering the open sea, and we haf reports of severe weather ahead. Haf a pleasant voyage."

The bare facts, unclothed by a single thread of reassurance. Even our most unlaconic emcee was momentarily speechless, and hints of sea-sick-green began to show on some faces there in the plush theatre.

Our seven-day cruise/family reunion netted many a memory: Lucullan meals splendidly served in the Manhattan dining room where the dress code usually suggested "elegantly casual" (or was it "casually elegant"?); sorting nostalgically with my sisters through our fondest childhood memories while watching spectacular skylines drift by; sipping chablis in the Crow's Nest while the sun slowly descended into a fiery merger with the Pacific, as a fine pianist ran deftly through *"Rhapsody in Blue."*

Henceforth, whenever I hear that Gershwin classic, it will flash images of spruce-covered mountain slopes, snow-strewn ridges, and a sunset pathway flaring across Alaskan waters.

"When you wake up tomorrow morning, we'll be anchored in Sitka," came an announcement one night while we were chatting in the Hudson Lounge. It aroused a tingle of anticipation, as we had half a day to roam this historic city, known in the old days as "The Paris of the Pacific."

Next morning I turned out before sunup, picked up that vital first cup of coffee in the Lido Restaurant, then stepped out on deck into softly lit enchantment. Sitka Sound encircled us with its necklace of islands silhouetted against the dawn. Arising out of low-hanging swirls of mist, each isle seemed miraculously suspended in mid-air. It was Coleridge's "Painted Ocean" there in the early stillness, save for the gentle wake trailing a few vessels that were stealing out to sea. One craft's name caught my fancy—*The Wind-Walker.* Soon the sleek, light blue *Cloud Nine* floated by, followed by a chugging, scarred, and weary fishing boat with the no-nonsense name, *The John Moore.*

I lingered at the rail, savoring the java and the bracing air and the shining serenity. Gradually the ghostly islands came into clearer focus, and the slow spread of sunlight set the trails of mist and Sitka's faraway buildings agleam. Never had I felt more keenly alive in every pore!

Then, out onto the deck and into my meditation, pranced a trim, male jogger. Apparently impervious to the enchanting atmosphere, he immediately leaned into a brisk stride up the starboard deck and bobbed out of sight. But he soon re-entered the scene, trotting down the port side, curving around the stern, and pressing on in determined circles around the 700-foot deck.

The eager jogger seemed oblivious to the phantom island necklace surrounding us, to the intensifying spread of yellow-orange down the slope of the coastal range, and to the graceful *Wind-Walker* skimming the still waters. He seemed conscious solely of his pace, the hostile minutes and seconds, and the runway immediately ahead. His pumping arms and legs expressed purposeful vigor. And yet, was there a hint of grimness in his body English? Was he over-straining to catch up with something? Or to escape something? Somehow, his persistent action seemed out of place in that entrancing atmosphere—like someone sweating through aerobics in the ethereal hush of a cathedral on a Sunday morning.

On the other hand, I thought as I headed for the Lido and a refill of coffee, maybe he's feeling something as deep and inspiring as I'm experiencing—a soaring sense of fitness that comes with deep-drawing lungs and well-worked muscles and stepped-up flow of blood.

In retrospect, "Kuuurrr—Whooooock!" was a standout experience. But far more profound and enduring were the sights, sensations, and silence of a Sitka sunrise. With that dawning, arose a powerful reminder, in sunrise colors, of the wondrous privilege in having a place in the sun—in just being alive!

And such a revelation can come upon us whether we are meditating in the morning quietude, pounding down a runway, or merely pausing at Main and Third to take stock of things.

CLASS REUNIONS—
A TIME FOR ALL BIRDS TO SING

Burlington, Iowa High School Class of '36—that was us! To the purple passages of "Pomp and Circumstance," we marched out fifty-eight years ago into the "Threadbare Thirties," with the world in the cruel clutches of the Great Depression.

We were awash back then in the alphabet soup of "CCC," "WPA," "HOLC," and many other New Deal agencies formed by FDR and his "Brain Trust," in desperate effort to resuscitate a moribund economy. A wistful slogan was circulating then, trying to ignite a little light for dark times: "Prosperity is just around the corner"—to which my witty father made a slight revision: "Prosperity is just around the *coroner.*"

Now, almost six decades later, we old grads gathered for our 58th reunion. Some arrived with slow shuffle. A few labored in on cane or crutch. Others made their entrance with fairly brisk stride. And the question was always hovering close to the warm greetings and embraces: "Why is life so kind to some, and so cruel to others?!"

Class reunions sharpen your appreciation for such basics as sight, hearing, and your original issue of teeth, hip joints, and knee joints. And, most of all, your appreciation for survival! Eighty-nine names appear on the *"In Memoriam"* page of our address book, out of a class of 250—and two more died in the brief interval between printing and distribution!

In my high school years, I found that courage, as well as prosperity, was extremely elusive. My first, full-fledged date was on graduation night. It was a blind date with an out-of-town girl—an awkward experience for me, and surely a boring one for her. But at least I was able to wax romantic afterwards, with my typewriter. I wrote her and boldly described how beautiful a blond girl looked in a white coat, in the blaze of moonlight over the Mississippi River. Her response was blunt and brief: "It was a *blue* coat."—Thus ended my first shy venture into romance!

While there was plenty of evidence of faltering memory at our reunion, most of us vividly recalled the soaring moments of victory on gym floor and playing field: glory-filled times of winning blue ribbons, golden trophies, conference championships.

But even more vivid in my memory is a brief interlude devoid of triumph and glory. A stubby-legged member of our track team just didn't have the right stuff for distance running. He almost always finished last; sometimes, *way* last! But he hung in there, through the entire track season.

At one track meet, having finished my events, I was standing at the finish line when this persistent fighter against mediocrity came trudging down the final stretch—a lonely runner on an empty track. Not a single cheer encouraged the solitary competitor, but how well I remember one, jeering, insensitive voice: "Hey fella, the race is over!" The close look I had at his face when he plodded across the line continues to haunt me: the mix of determination and despair...the mix of sweat and tears. I felt a powerful surge of sympathy—and a far more powerful surge of admiration for a blue-ribbon kind of courage.

When I described this enduring memory to my daughter-in-law who teaches at a Blackfeet school in Montana, she repeated a Native American saying...

> *If only the best birds would sing,*
> *The world would be a quiet place.*

More and more, we old grads come to realize that winning isn't everything; that there's also much to admire in losing.

An autumnal kind of mellowness comes flowing in to tone down our competitiveness. We think far less of winning out over others, and far more of winning out over the ignoble tendencies within ourselves. While growing older, we like to think that we're growing a little wiser, a little nicer, less bent on success and status. And, at least in one way, our vision and hearing improve with age, for we come to discern more clearly a rich quality and diversity in the people and voices around us.

I'm all out for class reunions. I'll keep coming, as long as I'm able. Because I've found that at old grad gatherings, we not only catch up on one another's lives, we bolster and brighten one another's lives. We deepen our gratitude for survival. And the glow of camaraderie encourages—not just the best birds—but *all* birds to SING!

FOR A BUOYANT BODY AND SOUL...

Swimming and I—what a cold-hot-cold-hot relationship we've had down through the years.

My earliest memory of venturing into water beyond bathtub depth is of a family frolic on a Mississippi River beach in Iowa. Both fun and fear were in that pre-kindergarten adventure: fun when I was in waist-deep water, and fear when I dared wade to shoulder-depth. I'd then beat a retreat to the friendly shallows and enviously watch my father and older siblings swimming joyously out there in the awesome depths.

Then came the YMCA Learn-To-Swim Campaign. Climbing the steps of the Y entrance was like mounting to the guillotine. But sensitive instructors helped the fun to override fear, and I was soon dog paddling around with growing confidence. But I drifted into the danger zone near the diving board, and a chunky lad belly-flopped onto me and I sank like a stone. I was swiftly hauled out, but all my confidence had drowned; it took quite a while to resuscitate it and again get it breathing on its own.

Then began a long phase when swimming was the most exciting thing on my horizon. What a thrill to branch out into different strokes, to launch into daring dives, to lunge into the crawl stroke and try to outdo Johnnie Weismuller, the star swimmer of that era. What anticipation when headed for the Y pool, or the beach on "Ol' Man River," or the swimmin' hole on Flint Creek!

But somewhere along the line, that passion cooled down as interest in baseball, tennis, handball and other sports heated up. My enthusiasm for things aquatic remained cold for decades...until our neighbors asked, "Ever thought of joining MASA?"

"What's MASA?" we asked.

"Marathon Area Swimming Association," they explained.

"With a membership, you can swim seven days a week in an Olympic-sized pool."

My spouse was instantly eager to take the plunge, but I felt no yen to get my feet wet. The next morning she accompanied our neighbors to the pool and returned with wet hair and a glowing report.

"It's wonderful! You swim laps for a warmup, then you're led through forty-five minutes of water exercises. What a GREAT feeling!"

Her enthusiasm impressed me, but next time she still went solo—and returned with a report that outglowed her first one. So I accompanied her on her third visit, and my lukewarm attitude began warming up when I met the cordial staff, shucked off my duds, showered, and entered the pool area. My enthusiasm rose to the simmering stage when I shoved off into the blue-green water, and felt that magical buoyancy and liquidity enveloping me. With a scissors kick I accelerated my glide, then thought again of surpassing Johnnie Weismuller— and let the thought pass.

Several times weekly at 8 A.M., rain or shine, below or above zero, we head for "The Beach," enjoying the sharp silhouette of wooded hills against the sunrise. We senior MASA members are all shapes and sizes, and we seem to share a desire to keep, or get, into shape. A few folk hobble painfully to the poolside, but once water-borne, their infirmities seem to dissolve away.

Water exercises are unbeatable for their benefit. Every movement under water meets resistance and your muscles—all of them—soon announce that they're being worked. Yet it's a gentle sort of workout, and rhythmically done to background music of Glenn Miller, Cole Porter, and George Gershwin.

"Now—swing that leg through figure eights," commands our leader. "Considering inflation," I asked, "shouldn't we be doing figure nines?"—We continued with the eights.

Our leaders ease us into a workout that gradually increases the pulse beat. They skillfully encourage us to "give it the old college try"—well, anyway the old post-graduate try—by deftly mixing fun with serious purpose. They administer a guaranteed remedy for stepping up your spirits and stepping down your tendinitis.

When you head for the showers after a watery workout, a feeling of well-being patters along with you. The only undesirable side effect is that when you return home at mid-morning, you're thinking about a hefty second breakfast, followed by a bit of a snooze. But when you're free, over 21, and retired, ain't no law sez you can't.

In the recent past, a bit of a health problem kept me high and dry-docked for a month. When I finally plunged back into MASA's waters, how exhilarating to feel again that buoyancy, that immersion in soothing liquidity! And I felt immersed, too, in a warm camaraderie: "Hey, welcome back." "We missed you. Everything okay?" "Good to see you, and I've got a picture of my newest grandson to show you."—Plunging once again into that friendly atmosphere brought as much buoyancy as gliding off into sparkling waters.

How long since you've tried a stint of water-borne exercise? Fitness experts say there's no better all-around workout for the old bod. And it's even better for the old psyche.

Once you take the plunge, you'll probably be saying to others, "C'mon in, the water's fine!"—Why not give it a swirl?

VOICES FROM

CHRISTMAS PAST

"...IF ONLY IN MY DREAMS"

"You can't go home again," declared that writer of the '30s, Thomas Wolfe. But at Christmas time, many of us *do* go home again, "if only in our dreams," as that wistful seasonal song says. Poignant memories overwhelm us, and we find ourselves wandering through those vanished times when our children were very young, and when we, ourselves, were very young.

Every late December I relive an evening of my childhood when I was startled into near-delirium at the sight of Santa bursting through our front door with a tale about his sleigh breaking down outside. "Santa," I later learned, was a jovial, overweight friend of my father's, but I swallowed that sham—hook, line and reindeer! There are some who frown on the Santa stuff today, but if it scarred my psyche in any way, I'm unaware of it. The myth has brought me many a bright flashback. And even after I wised up, I went through more than one Christmas pretending that I still believed, so that I wouldn't bruise my parents' feelings.

Before sunup on Christmas day my mother would be in her kitchen preparing Danish delicacies. And for an agonizing time we four youngsters would be confined to the upstairs where our father, "The General," would prepare his troops for "The March to the Christmas Tree." He'd line us up, order us to count off, march, and reverse march. Then he'd lead us downstairs at tantalizingly slow pace, circle us through the front hall where we could barely glimpse the tree ablaze in the living room, march us through the kitchen and into the dining room, then reverse march us back through kitchen and hall. Finally, at the living room entrance, when our suspense was building toward explosion, he'd give the command to "break ranks" and we'd stampede to the tree.

How vividly it all comes back, season after season: the

soaring suspense, the fragrance of coffee and bacon and eggs-a-la-goldenrod, the breath-stopping sight of new ice skates, a new Flexible Flyer sled promising supersonic flight, and my mother's and father's faces just beyond the lights and tinsel, bright with the joy they found in our joy.

Another vision returns each Holiday—the faces of our own youngsters, aglow with excitement, or revealing a more subdued light when singing in the children's Christmas choir. The solemn intensity of a child, caught up in the spell of music, is a thing of beauty.

While listening to my son and his grade school class, singing carols in public performance years ago, I felt the full surge of the Christmas Spirit. I couldn't help but note how one lad's voice overpowered all the others, due to its awesomely resounding monotone. Yet, the boy appeared to be in near-rapture as he lost himself in his dissonant noise. He was pouring his all into something wonderful and mysterious, and if beauty was utterly lacking in his one-note noise, it was shining in his eyes and upturned face.

One Christmas Eve in church brought a similar experience when listening to the organist's prelude. "Prof" Krueger had presided at our organ for many decades. The snow-haired bachelor's whole life had revolved around music, and his pale-blue eyes had the faraway look of one who listens to those "sweeter, unheard melodies" that resounded in the fine ear of the poet, John Keats.

But in his later years, "Prof" was beginning to lose his touch, and an occasional wrong note would jar the musical flow. That Christmas Eve, when wincing at one of the discords, I got to thinking about the old gentleman's long career—about his lifelong dedication to music. And I began listening to him with all my mind and heart, rather than ear alone, and the sour notes dissolved into sweet harmony—an unmarred consonance that wasn't really there.

Another Christmas season similarly featured a kind of beauty that wasn't actually there. My wife and I had returned from a holiday gathering to find a singularly frowsy wreath on our table. Our children explained that a stranger had rapped on our door and announced: "Here's the wreath your folks ordered. It costs five dollars." Understandably taken in, our youngsters fetched the money, paid for the sad glob of tired evergreen and crumbly pine cones, and the wreath peddler vanished into the night.

We had ordered no wreath, so why didn't I report the fraud? Perhaps it was the Christmas Spirit that restrained me. Or maybe it was our children's description of the stranger: "He was awful old and grey, and his clothes were awful, and he seemed awful sad," they reported. And the longer that scruffy wreath was with us through that season, the more we came to sense a certain beauty in it that wasn't really there. The magic of Christmas!

One special Christmas tree gleams in memory—a tree that wasn't really there. A lush, symmetrical, thirty-five dollar balsam? No—a very old wild cherry that stood outside our living room window. The old-timer was leaning arthritically to leeward, its arteries hardened, its red-bronze trunk ravaged by time. We were about to fell it, but decided to keep it with us through one last Christmas Season.

The tree had been young and lithe once, and it grew up with our children. It shaded all of Kathleen's and Christine's fanciful sandpile sculpturings. Young Phil would shinny to its top for a view of the larger world. Randy hung a trapeze from a lower limb and enjoyed many a free-swinging hour. Our collie slumbered through her final days in the soft stir of its leaves. Through all our holidays, the tree had been there within our lamplight glow—a sentinel at the golden border of Christmas.

We were glad that we'd have our gnarled friend with us

for one last season, with stars flaring their silver through its stark branches. We'd think about how a tree is not merely roots and trunk and branches, but a thousand, gently-rustling memories.

Alas, in mid-December an insensate wind swept in to rampage through the night, and in the grey dawn we discovered that our venerable sentinel had been "put down."

While we enjoyed our colorful inside tree that Christmas, we kept glancing out at the lonesome space beyond our window, where once stood a not-so-fancy tree whose branches had been intertwined with a countless host of priceless memories.

Of all the yesterdays that come rushing back at Christmas time, the most vivid one is a morning brilliant with new snow and sunlight. On that cloudless day, we had driven our youngsters out to the ski hill, enjoying their excited chatter about the downhill adventure awaiting them. They hurried into their gear and headed for the tow line as we stood and watched them go, their small figures sharply silhouetted against a background of sunlit snow. Midway they paused, looked back and waved, then double-poled eagerly onward.

That vision's final scene is of our children gliding upward on the tow, slowly receding into snowy distance. And just at that moment, the strains of "Silver Bells" came floating out from the chalet, ringing through the brisk air.

Ever since, whenever and wherever we hear that Christmas ballad, all the radiance of that long ago moment is instantly rekindled—an expanse of new snow glistening in morning sunlight—young voices chiming in excitement—young faces glowing in frosty air. And the silhouettes of four children, gliding slowly upward and away in eager ascent, fading off into high adventure.

SHIFTING INTO THE GOODWILL GEAR

Roads, drivers, the whole world take on a different look this time of year. Most drivers don't seem in such an all-fired hurry during the Christmas Season. There are so many more smiles behind windshields; so many more friendly waves as motorists invite others to take a left turn in front of them, or allow them to squeeze in ahead, when traffic is bumper-to-bumper.

The grim determination to get there fast doesn't seem to obsess nearly as many as it does in pre and post-Christmas times. It's heartwarming to see what happens within our world of wheels when there's a bit of goodwill with us in the driver's seat!

How great it would be if the Christmas Spirit remained within our human traffic clear around the calendar. Think of all the sprung hoods, the bashed-in bumpers, the ill will in four-wheeled motion that we'd prevent if we drove through *all* seasons with Christmas kindness in our hearts!

We'd spread far more human warmth than exhaust fumes along the traffic lanes if we drove congenially like Santa Claus, rather than like one of the Unsers at the Indianapolis 500. Think of the far-reaching example we'd set if we always tried to give fellow drivers a break, rather than force them to brake.

Considerate driving might cost us a few extra seconds—but who can't spare a few seconds!? Beware and pity those who just can't spare the time; they're driving through life with a grossly exaggerated sense of self-importance. The bigger the ego, the more rude and dangerous the driving performance!

That gentle genius, Albert Einstein, observed that "No one who is in a hurry is quite civilized." How often have you seen an uncivilized eager-weaver whiz by you—and a few minutes later you find him a mere car length or two ahead of you at a red light?

What a wonderful thing it would be if we could all manage to keep the spirit of Santa Claus and Albert Einstein with us permanently in the driver's seat...and in the seat of our minds. Kindness and goodwill are the most precious of cargoes to carry with us down every path we travel, both on wheels and afoot. How great it would be—what a different world it would be—if all of us managed to shift permanently into the goodwill gear!

RE-AWAKENING

The bleakness of that wind-ravaged December day had seeped into my spirits, I guess. Or perhaps it was because I had trudged about in vain search for a particular Christmas gift. Whatever the cause, the Spirit was not with me as I threaded my way through the teeming aisles of one more store.

I then found myself in the colorful clutter of the toy department—and there on an elevated throne was King Santa, in rich-red outfit and freshly drycleaned beard. He seemed a lonesome figure just then, for shoppers were clustered around a store employee who was putting an electric train through its paces. It was late evening, and fatigue-lines were beginning to dominate over the laughter-wrinkles on Santa's face. He yawned, then lapsed into a cheerless stare at his fur-tipped boots.

"You're not the man you used to be, Santa," I thought. "The old magic is long gone. You're just a commercial old elf, bent on filling the merchants' stockings with profits. You're the plump star of the nation's greatest sales push, and the jingle of Donner's and Blitzen's harness bells is overwhelmed by the cash register's jangle. No, Santa, you're not what you used to be."

Then a small voice wedged its sharp excitement into my reflections. "Mommie, Santee Claus—Lo-o-ok!" Her words echoed throughout the toy department. The weary sag went out of Santa's frame, and genuine wrinkles of kindness appeared on his face. The tiny lass was momentarily frozen in rapture—a graceful little statue, pointing out her breathtaking discovery. Then she broke away from her mother and bounded toward the enthroned, legendary figure. Partway there, she paused uncertainly, then continued with skips of shy eagerness.

Gently encouraged by her mother, the child finally stepped onto the platform and stood with hands clasped together, her shining eyes studying the fabulous fellow so near to her, her diminutive frame rigid with excitement, and wonder, and hope.

As I studied her uplifted face, dusty childhood sensations came alive within me, rising on a wave of tenderness. And when I walked away, some of the old Christmas embers were once again aglow inside...and over the store's tumult I seemed to hear the faint tinkle of reindeer harness bells.

"Forgive me, Santa," I thought. "It's been a long time, but how well I remember! You're still the same as you used to be. You'll *always* be the same!"

TRANSFORMATION

Strange how things change so suddenly! Take the winter cold. Yesterday it was a bitter, bullying thing, gnawing at you relentlessly. Today it's a crispness that brings your head up high and starts a tingling in your blood. It puts snap in your stride and sparkle in your eye.

Then there's the snow. A short while ago it was an infernal nuisance. You were weary of its glitter; weary of trudging through it. Now there's a glistening whiteness that wasn't there before—and it's taken all the barrenness out of the landscape.

There's transformation everywhere you look—from frosty dawn to ruddy sunset. And beyond the sunset, too! The stars have unusual brightness in their gleam.

Home has a new snugness about it; a warmer welcome in the look of its threshold. Light streams from its windows to flood the snow with pathways of yellow-gold, gleaming in the dusk. With glad heart and eager footsteps you hasten to your door.

And—wonder of wonders—even people have changed! They've lost their annoying ways. Gone is the fretful crossfire and friction. Friendly harmony rules. Smiles, with real feeling in them, greet you on every hand. Come to think of it, *you*, too, radiate the same, spontaneous warmth! There's new tenderness within your family circle, drawing you closer together.

What is this miracle that has worked such startling changes in us and our world? It's a pause from the all-absorbing hustle of getting ahead to marvel at the beauty of sunset, and stars, and human kindness. It's a return to youthful enthusiasms. It's a reappearance of our "Sunday best," from its closeting deep within our being, adorning us all for a brief winter's spell.

But most of us call it, "The Spirit of Christmas."

THE CHRISTMAS QUEST

Somewhere in the blithe heart of Christmas Eve, a vague discontent steals over us, bringing pause to our gaiety and sending us like questing children to a vigil at the window.

Turning from the festive glow, we search the lonely sweep of stars for something above and beyond the tinseled pleasures and Santa Claus delights.

And, if we search with the soul's keen vision, perhaps we will find what we seek. It will have more splendor than all earth's Christmas lights and candles. It will be as distant as the North Star, and as close as your heart. It will be as ancient as the expanse of nearly two thousand years, and as young as this very Christmas Eve. It will gleam among the shadows of eternity, and it will adorn your earthly being with the evergreen of hope and the celestial ornaments of goodwill.

It is a wondrous thing to look deep into the face of the Silent Night, and to find at last, in the timelessness beyond the stars, the Spirit of Christmas.

I'm more than just a gaudy show
Of red, and green, and tinsel-shine.
I'm more than steaming, festive food
And clustered gifts in wrappings, fine.

I fling a brightness o'er the heart;
A gleam of star-shine from the night.
I drape good will around the world
And trim humanity with light.

GRACE FOR CHRISTMAS

We are thankful for a world of wondrous things:

For flame of winter dawns...soft spread of snow...
the white star-fire of winter nights.

For talents which have brought to us this food,
this home, this glowing warmth.

For family love—the strength and stabilizer of
our lives.

For the familiar blessings of today; the hope and
unknown promise of tomorrow.

For the constant whisper in our minds, spurring us
on toward higher thoughts and deeds.

And we are thankful, most of all, for the One who
brought the Christmas Spirit to the world, urging us
to keep Good Will aglow, not as a brief winter's flame,
but as a constant splendor.

ANGEL CHIMES

He was a small boy—but with large imagination—and when he wriggled into bed at the close of Christmas day, bright visions began flashing through his darkened room.

He thought of the dazzling tree that had brought magic to his home. He relived the suspense of tearing open many, mysterious packages. He saw once more the glitter, the gaiety, the Santa Claus images that had flitted across the television screen. His mind scouted in drowsy pleasure to the tractor with the real gearshift...to the ice skates that were going to speed him into flight...to the cowboy hat that was just like the ones the good guys wore when they galloped off after the bad guys.

But soon those boisterous thoughts faded, and out of the day's excitement came a far different vision. There was the orange spurt of a match at the dinner table...the gleam of candles, touched off one by one under the "Angel Spelet"—the Swedish Angel Chimes...the slow, starting spiral of the winged trio, trumpets at their lips...and then, as they flew faster and faster, scarcely-heard music had drifted upon the silence as the chimes were brushed by the swinging pendants.

Snug under his blankets, the boy again experienced the wondrousness of those moments. He thought of his mother's smile in the soft play of candlelight; the sparkle in his sister's eyes as she watched the angel flight; the words of grace his father had spoken, intermingled with the gentle tinkling of the chimes. Once more he sensed the warmth of something tremendous and unknown that had swept over him, there in the hushed room.

At last the boy's eyes closed in the darkness and he was borne across slumber's border upon the wings of angelic harmony—a blend of pure chimes, pure thoughts, pure feelings that captured some of the splendor of winter stars...some of the awe of a Silent Night long ago in Bethlehem...some of the radiance of human love that is the spirit—the very soul—of Christmas.

AFTERWORD

I turn, at last, to listen to the most distant of voices—those two that were the very first to enter my stream of consciousness: the voices of my mother and my father.

We were four, fortunate children who grew up in a warm and lively home. We had the normal quota of dark and stormy stretches, but our parents were remarkable providers of contentment and free-flowing talk. They cultivated a magical ambiance that soothed away trouble, anger and fear.

The protagonist of our circle was our father. But mother, too, occasionally stepped onto center stage with a witticism or vigorous rebuttal. She would, at times, launch into sharp criticism of someone, and Dad would try to gentle things with a Dickensian line: "Now Lee, remember: 'We're all poor critters.'" But seldom would either Dickens or Dad succeed in softening her mood.

Mother's parents had both migrated from Denmark, and she was quite proud of her Danish lineage. She would sometimes needle Dad about his German/"Dutch-Doodle" ancestry, and he would retaliate with: "You darn Danes came into England and burned down all the libraries!"

Mother put herself through business college and worked as a bookkeeper before her marriage. She was a whiz at things mathematical, and that particular gene of hers never made it into my chromosomic collection.

Our mother had a strong instinct for neatness and order, which was evident in her cupboards, her closets, her entire household. Yet, there wasn't a glimmer of cold formality in our home; instead there was that all-enveloping ambiance, encouraging us to relax and *enjoy!*

Legia Inge (Hansen) Carspecken—the name brings instantly into focus a vision of my mother in crisp white apron, hands snowy with flour, fingers deftly shaping pie crust or pastry, face in serious concentration on the blending of visual beauty with exquisite taste and nourishment.

Our mother nourished us, not only with painstakingly planned menus, but with such a stubborn spirit and courage that we called her "Danish dander." We never saw her cry, and though not given much to an outward show of affection, she kept a kindly light aglow in her blue-grey eyes. She was always with us in support and encouragement, no matter how far we roamed or how badly we blundered.

She was always first up in the morning, and as she launched into the new day, faint sounds would drift gently into our consciousness to dissolve our slumber: soft rustlings as she dressed; her brisk step on the stairway; the opening of doors and drawers far down in her kitchen; the muted percussion of pots and pans; the nearly inaudible clink of silverware on her table; the teakettle's shrill announcement. And finally, a coffee/bacon/toast fragrance soaring into our bedrooms, along with a cheery "Time to get up!" In such a harmonious way, she set our world in motion for us at each daybreak—and those gentle rhythms are a part of our pulse beat today.

Laughter was common in our home, and it would erupt in full volume at mother's unintentional spoonerisms (transposing the initial sounds of words). When dining one evening with our minister and his wife, the former remarked that he'd seen a church member's name in the paper, "but I can't remember what for." "Oh, I know," Mother said. "He was arrested for pussing in a bark zone."

This gene of hers I *did* inherit. My most recent bit of unintentional spoonerizing occurred on a cafeteria line, where I startled the attendant behind the counter by asking for "the nuna toodle casserole."

Our mother's mind remained clear and inquiring until nearly the end. While conversing with her in her 94th year, I mentioned mental telepathy. "Ah-ah," she said, shaking her head, "you're being redundant. Telepathy *is* a mental process." As for her "Danish dander," it diminished somewhat, but some embers were still aglow, up to the last.

And how do I sum up the protagonist of our family circle? Our father was a businessman/athlete/poet/philosopher/scholar/romanticist/outdoorsman/provider, with a bubbling zest for life. Rheumatic fever cut short his formal education at the sixth grade, but he read avidly, methodically built an impressive vocabulary, learned shorthand and became a court reporter, and, with his earliest wages, began to buy sets of Shakespeare, Dickens, Mark Twain, and other classics. The works of the English romantic poets were among his top favorites.

Our father set out to study law, and then diverged into the abstracting profession. He started an abstract company, struggled mightily to build it and keep it alive through the "threadbare thirties," and in spare time managed to pour his wide-ranging thoughts into prose and poetry. He often recited his original verse around the house, and we children came to know many a line by heart. In grade school, I was caught unprepared after our teacher had asked us to select and memorize a poem in our textbook. When she unexpectedly called upon me to recite, I stood and repeated the only lines that entered my panicked brain:

> There is no death, the poet says;
> Then why the undertaker?
> Then why the tombstone artisan,
> And why the coffin-maker?
> They put us in the cold, cold ground
> And heap the clods upon it.
> There is no death, the poet says;
> He's talkin' through his bonnet!

"Who in the world wrote that?" asked my wide-eyed teacher. "My father," I announced with pride.

Dad also found time to roam the great out-of-doors, fishing the Mississippi River and its southeastern Iowa tributaries, and later the lakes of western Ontario's Quetico Park. He wrote vivid accounts of his adventures and impressions in a local newspaper column, *"Verse 'n Worse,"* and a friend persuaded him to publish a collection of his writing in a book, *"Fishin' Poems and Others,"* which circulated widely without benefit of professional promotion.

We offspring especially remember our father's indomitable optimism. Even through that stark period when the great depression ravaged his business, and the persistent threat of angina dogged him, his brown eyes never lost their sparkle. He greeted each dawn with poetry and song, delivered with gusto! What a role model he was for us—and continues to be—with his buoyant humor, irrepressible wit and searching mind.

I will forever be haunted by one of the last statements I heard my father utter. His final years were not good ones, and near the end I tried reminiscing with him over our Canadian wilderness adventures. "Remember that wonderful campsite of ours on Lake Agnes?" I asked. "Just around the bend from Louisa Falls?"—And then that haunting expression registered upon his face, a mixture of confusion and regret and wistfulness. And his faltering words: "Lake Agnes? I—I can't remember...but—I think that sometimes I see it in my dreams."

I hope that our father's final dream, this side of the divide, was of Lake Agnes, or of another one of the wild places that he loved. After his death, in fulfillment of his wishes, his ashes were scattered along one of his favorite Mississippi River sloughs—one of the many sylvan sanctuaries that nourished and renewed him.

The night of our father's death, I walked outside into the dark to think about things—about the meaning and evanescence of life—about how a whole world, a secure and contented family circle, a home glowing with a magic, indefinable ambiance, could have vanished—could have dissolved away in the inexorable, downstream flow of time!

Out there in the darkness, I began to struggle for some kind of words, thoughts, to send somewhere out into the boundless unknown:

> ALONE, out in the vast night of your death,
> I searched the skies we star-struck two once roamed,
> And sighted but a misty-silver blur, until...
> Dim at the edge, appeared The Pleiades,
> And then I seemed to glimpse a ghostly trace
> Of smoke from our old campfires.
>
> I thought of you, outdistancing infirmity
> With eager stride, as on your beckoning trails,
> The old zest shining in your eyes,
> And ringing through your voice.
>
> You are far beyond my known horizons, now.
> And yet—the distant Pleiades still brightly gleam
> As long ago, when you first guided me
> To their six, silvery points of fire,
> And the seventh, scarcely seen.
> The rhythms of your poetry still flow.
> Your sunrise songs still echo in my mind.
>
> My world's enriched by all you centered on:
> Good writing and good music and good talk;
> The silent sermons flowing through the dawn;
> The wonder of deep lakes, deep woods, deep sky—
> And deeper mystery now engulfing you.

We offspring arranged for the planting of two young conifers in a hometown park to memorialize the lives of our parents. Nowadays, when we visit the site, we feel uplifted to see these vigorous evergreens, reaching eagerly outward and upward toward the sun. When a wind sifts through their boughs, we hear once more the soothing music that our mother and our father created and kept flowing through our home. We sense again the warmth and contentment of that vanished ambiance which once enveloped us.

And, even on windless days, if we listen hard enough, we finally hear, deep in the stillness, the same reassuring music—the same reassuring voices.

Both the author and publisher of VOICES FROM DOWNSTREAM express their appreciation for permission to use the author's writings which previously had appeared in the following publications:

AMERICAN FORESTS, published by The American Forestry Association, Washington DC

WISCONSIN, The Sunday Magazine of The Milwaukee Journal Sentinel, Milwaukee, WI.

THE ROTARIAN, published by Rotary International, Evanston, IL.

AFTER HOURS, published by Wausau Insurance Companies, Wausau, WI.

WISCONSIN, published by Wisconsin Trails/Tamarack Press, Madison, WI.